SPRING HARVEST 2014
THEME GUIDE

MALCOLM DUNCAN

Your daily guide to exploring Unbelievable

Spring Harvest wishes to acknowledge and thank the following people for their help in the compilation and production of this theme guide:

The Spring Harvest Planning Group - Pete Broadbent, Malcolm Duncan, Abby Guinness, Virginia Luckett, Ian Macdowell, Cathy Madavan, Peter Martin, Cris Rogers & Paul Weston.

Steph Adam, Maria Bond, Rebecca Bowater, Jaqs Graham, Denise Hooper, Emma Howden, Steve May-Miller & Alice O'Kane.

TIPS ON HOW TO USE THE THEME GUIDE

The Unbelievable Theme Guide is easy to use and is designed so you can use it as an individual or in a small group. It will help you to reflect on the teaching and material you engage with during Spring Harvest 2014. It will also help you to bring Spring Harvest back to your local church or context and continue to explore some of the things that we have been looking at during your time at Spring Harvest.

The Theme Guide this year has been designed to complement the Spring Harvest day effectively and to help you to identify the single theme of the whole day so that you can see the connections across everything that is going on.

To help you get the best out of the Theme Guide during your time at Spring Harvest (and when you get back home), each day's material sits alongside the various meetings, teaching, spaces and celebrations that will be taking place during the day.

We've included some simple symbols so that you can easily find your place in the Theme Guide and some suggestions for session recordings you might want to order to take home with you. The material in the various sessions of the day and the Theme Guide will work hand-in-hand to equip you, your small group and your church so that you can have greater confidence in God and realise just how much confidence God has in you.

Fitting It All Together

When you see this symbol it means that these sections will give you a helpful and quick summary of how the material across the whole day fits together.

Let's Get Started

This symbol means that these sections will give you a helpful summary of some of the ideas that are being covered in the Big Start. They aren't exactly the same, but they are along the same lines.

Think About It

Sections marked with this symbol will give you a helpful summary of some of the ideas that are being covered in the Bible Study. Don't expect it to be exactly the same – nothing replaces being there to hear the teaching, but it will help you to see where the Bible Study fits into the rest of the day and how the themes we are exploring flow out of our exploration of the truths contained in the Apostles' Creed.

Digging Deeper

This is the largest section in the Theme Guide, and will help you to think through the idea behind each day by looking at the theme through the lens of the particular 'Space' you are interested in. This section will help you to apply the truth of what you are learning to the situations you are most interested in or find yourself in most often. Remember, we have replaced 'Learning Zones' (which were based on your learning style) with 'Spaces' (which are based on the things you are facing or the situations you find yourself in most often or are most interested in.)

Encountering God

When you see this symbol it means that this section will help you to connect the Evening Celebrations with the rest of the day and will help you to think about ways in which you can both PREPARE to meet with God in a celebration and REFLECT on what God has done in a celebration afterwards.

Take Away

Sections marked with this symbol are built around some questions and reflections for you to explore either as an individual, in small groups or as a church family. It will help you to continue the journey that you have begun this week, and will be really helpful as you go home for you and for the wider church family you are part of. It includes details of some of the session recordings you might find helpful.

Prayer And Reflection

When you see this symbol it means that this section has resources that can help you think and pray and connect with God in an act of worship, meditation, reflection or through one of the spiritual disciplines.

Hungry For More

This symbol means that you can read more about this idea or section in *Unbelievable: Confident Faith In A Sceptical World* by Malcolm Duncan

Six tips on how to use the Theme Guide.

The Unbelievable Theme Guide will help you across all of Spring Harvest and beyond. Don't buy a Theme Guide and let it sit on your coffee table or bedside cabinet! It's a great resource, not just for when you are at Celebrations and in the Spaces, but also when you are in your chalet or trying to catch a few minutes to think and pray. It's also a great resource for you to take back home and use with other Christians. Here are six simple ideas on how to use it.

One
During your time at Spring Harvest, use the sections marked 'Take Away' as a devotional guide. Take a moment at the beginning and end of each day to reflect on the questions and use some of the prayers and resources to help you connect the material to your heart, not just your head.

Two
Before the Evening Celebrations, use the section on 'Encountering God' to prepare your heart for the meeting. Ask the Lord to do in you what he wants to do on that evening.

Three
If you are here as part of a group, try to talk about the 'Digging Deeper' sections. How did the theme of the day tie into the various Spaces? What can you learn from each other and how can you pray for one another?

Four
If you are a young person or a child, or you are here with young people and children, take a few minutes to talk across the generations about what God is saying to you. How can you encourage someone in another generation?

Five
Buy a couple of copies of the Theme Book, *Unbelievable: Confident Faith In A Sceptical World* by Malcolm Duncan and read it when you get home. Keep one and give one away.

Six
Work out how many people there are in your church, buy them each a copy of the Unbelievable Theme Guide and use it as a small group resource or study book when you get home.

Grab a coffee and get started...

Contents

Getting to grips with the theme

SOMETIMES WE THINK THE GOSPEL IS TOO GOOD TO BE TRUE!

GRACE IS LOVE THAT SEEKS YOU OUT WHEN YOU HAVE NOTHING TO GIVE IN RETURN.
GRACE IS LOVE COMING AT YOU THAT HAS NOTHING TO DO WITH YOU.
GRACE IS BEING LOVED WHEN YOU ARE UNLOVABLE.

Paul Zahl, *Grace In Practice*[1]

I BELIEVE, HELP MY UNBELIEF.

A desperate father who asked Jesus to help his son.[2]

1   ZAHL, Paul, Grace In Practice: A Theology Of Everyday Life,
(Grand Rapids: Wm B. Eerdmans Publishing Company, 2007).
2   The whole story is found in Mark 9:14-29, NB v. 24.

God is better than we think!

God is far kinder than we could ever dream of. He is far more beautiful. He is far more gracious. He is far more forgiving. He is far more willing to accept us as we are and change us than we are willing to accept him as he is. He loved us before we ever knew him[3] and his commitment to us is far stronger than our commitment to him[4]. He has dealt with the sin that separated us from him[5] and restored us to a right relationship with himself[6]. He has given us gifts so that we can serve him[7] and he has committed himself to producing his character in us[8]. He has committed to using the Church to show his purpose and beauty in the world[9] and to shining through us as we serve him[10]. He has promised to finish the work he has started in us[11] and he is fundamentally committed to the transformation of the whole planet.[12] The Good News isn't just a last ditch attempt to sort out my sin and failing, the Good News is good news for every person at every level. God is better than we could ever imagine!

For many people, the idea of this kind of God is just unbelievable. The concept of a loving, forgiving and self-sacrificing God is just too good to be true. We live in a culture that says that there is no such thing as a free lunch. We work hard and only want what we deserve and we definitely don't deserve this kind of God. In a society that believes you don't get anything for nothing we just can't understand the lavishness of God. There *must* be a catch in the Gospel, mustn't there? There has to be a secret clause somewhere, surely? Becoming a Christian must be a contract in which the small print that says that God will only love me if I clean up my act first and sort myself out, right? Wrong.

God is more than a big version of us

Most Christians find it difficult to believe the Gospel in its entirety. In an attempt to make God more manageable we domesticate his grace. We put far more conditions on his acceptance of us than he does. Over the years we accommodate our notions of having to earn God's love or having to do something to make sure that he *still* loves us. As a result, we begin to believe things that are clearly not true about him. For example, we think that there are some places that we can go, where God does not go – yet God himself makes it clear that he will never leave us[13], that there is nowhere that we can go where he is not present.[14] If we are not careful we end up distorting the Gospel because we are unable to cope with the sheer goodness of it. In distorting the Gospel, we distort God himself. For example, those of us who come from a 'protestant evangelical' tradition can fall into the terrible trap of having come to faith because we have discovered the grace of God, but living our Christian lives on the hamster-wheel of trying to please him. As another example, those of us who come from a Roman Catholic tradition can end up picturing God as an angry old man who delights in punishing his creation and who can never be pleased. Those of us who find our home in the charismatic traditions of the church can end up believing in a God who is only with us if we 'feel' him. The truth is that if we are not careful we all end up making God look like a pale version of who he really is. In the words of Brian McLaren:

ACCUMULATING ORTHODOXY MAKES IT HARDER, YEAR BY YEAR, TO BE A CHRISTIAN THAN IT WAS IN JESUS' DAY.

Brian McLaren, *A Generous Orthodoxy.*[15]

---

3   Romans 5:8.
4   1 John 4:19.
5   1 Peter 2:24.
6   Romans 8:14-17.
7   1 Corinthians 12.
8   Galatians 5:22-23.
9   Ephesians 3:10.
10   Matthew 5:13-17. Ephesians 2:10.
11   Philippians 1:6.
12   Habakkuk 2:14.

---

13   Deuteronomy 31:6; Hebrews 13:5.
14   Psalm 139:7-12.
15   McLaren, Brian, A Generous Orthodoxy: Why I Am A Missional + Evangelical + Post/Protestant + Liberal/Conservative + Mystical/ Poetic + Biblical + Charismatic/Contemplative + Fundamentalist/ Calvinist + Anabaptist/Anglican + Methodist + Catholic + Green + Incarnational + Depressed-Yet-Hopeful + Emergent + Unfinished Christian (Grand Rapids: Zondervan, 2004).

Avoiding the idol factory of our hearts.

John Calvin described the human heart as an idol factory, and commented that every one of us from our mother's womb is an expert in inventing idols. This is even true when it comes to our understanding of God. We would rather deal with the version of him that we can manage than the version of him that we cannot understand. There are two equally major mistakes that we can make when it comes to what we believe about God:

1. The Tyrannical God:
We believe that God can never be happy with us and therefore we always feel like a failure. We end up running away from God because we are constantly afraid of him. 'Church' is either a place for good people or a place that we go to so that we don't feel guilty.

2. The Anything-Goes God:
We think that our choices and lifestyles don't matter and that God approves of everything we do and everything we are. We end up defining 'Church' as nothing other than a nicer version of our communities or a place where choices don't matter, change isn't needed and we need never feel challenged.

Both of these mistakes have consequences for the way we think about ourselves as individuals, the Church as God's people and the place and role of the Church in the world. Yet there is also a third option.

3. The God Of The Gospel:
We allow our vision of God to be shaped by his utter beauty and goodness. We choose to believe what the Bible says about him, about us and about his church. We end up humbled by God's generosity, and 'Church' becomes a community where real change, and real hope, is possible. We become a community that shows our wider communities what God is like.

	Belief	Consequences		
		Ourselves	*The Church*	*The Church's role in the world*
1	*The Tyrannical God*	We are never good enough. We strive for perfection and punish ourselves when we make mistakes.	Guilt is a core feature of the Church. We don't often 'enjoy' church and we certainly don't 'enjoy' God. We emphasise TRUTH at the expense of GRACE.	The world is a place of darkness, sin and wickedness. Our job is to tell the world that 'they' need to change and to confront 'them' with 'their' sin.
2	*The Anything-Goes God*	We justify our actions and attitudes and never feel the need to change or be changed.	A lost sense of distinctiveness. The Church becomes nothing more than a mirror of the society in which we find ourselves. We emphasise GRACE at the expense of TRUTH.	The world is a place of beauty where notions such as 'sin' are old fashioned and outdated. The Church has no distinctive moral or ethical voice. Our job is to tell the world that God loves them and does not require change.
3	*The God Of The Gospel*	We know our own shortcomings but we also know what God is truly like. Our lives are viewed through the lenses of grace AND truth.	The Church is a collection of people who are called together to show the world what God is like. We are aware of our shortcomings, but we are also aware of God's character. We are a community that both 'knows' God and 'encounters' God. We are changed continually by God. We hold on to the joint principles of TRUTH and GRACE	The world is a place of great beauty AND great darkness, wickedness and sin. The Church is a community of people who demonstrate what God's heart is. We are called to demonstrate what a mutual commitment to authentic and transforming community can look like. We show the world that change is possible and that hope is real.

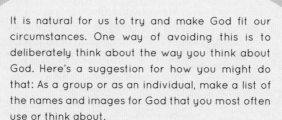

It is natural for us to try and make God fit our circumstances. One way of avoiding this is to deliberately think about the way you think about God. Here's a suggestion for how you might do that: As a group or as an individual, make a list of the names and images for God that you most often use or think about.

1. What is the source of those names and images?
2. Where are those names and images of God present in our traditions of Christianity?
3. To what extent are they life giving?
4. To what extent are they broken, distorted or distorting?

What do we really believe?

Michael Novak is an American, a philosopher and a Roman Catholic. In his book, *Belief & Unbelief: A Philosophy Of Self-Knowledge*,[16] he identifies three ways in which we 'believe' and hold our conviction:

Public Belief

This is what we want other people to think we believe, but we do not believe it. We may have a hidden agenda or some anxiety about what people will think of us if they knew what we really believed. Whatever the reason, we want people to think we believe something when we actually do not believe it at all.

An example of 'public belief' is the story of King Herod, who pretended to want to know where the baby Jesus was so that Herod could worship him, when the truth was that Herod actually wanted to kill Jesus.[17]

Private Belief

This is what we think we believe, but we actually do not believe it, because although we claim to believe it, and genuinely think we do believe it, we do not live it.

An example of this could be the story of King David and his adultery with Bathsheba. David genuinely believed that he was seeking to honour Yahweh, but his lifestyle and his beliefs contradicted one another.[18]

Core Belief

Core belief is what we really believe. It is not seen in what we say; it is seen in what we do. Our words flow out of our convictions, and our convictions shape our actions.

An example of this is the teaching of James in his epistle when he speaks of how we treat the poor.

He says that faith, without the accompanying demonstration of your convictions, is worthless.[19]

Margaret Thatcher became known as 'The Iron Lady' because of her tough approach to politics. The film of her life, released in 2011, was given that title. In the movie she is portrayed as a conviction-based politician. She is perhaps one of the most divisive characters in British politics. You either loved her, or hated her, but the one thing you could not do is be unclear about who she was or what she stood for.

In *The Iron Lady*, there is a scene when Margaret Thatcher goes to see her doctor. He asks her how she is 'feeling' and her repost is swift:

People don't think any more, they feel, "how are you feeling?", "Oh, I don't feel comfortable", "Oh, I'm so sorry, we, the group, we're feeling"... Do you know, one of the great problems of our age is that we are governed by people who care more about feelings than they do about thoughts and ideas. Now, thoughts and ideas, they interest me... Watch your thoughts, for they become words. Watch your words, for they become actions. Watch your actions, for they become habits. Watch your habits, for they become your character. Watch your character, for it becomes your destiny.
Margaret Thatcher in *The Iron Lady*[20]

We become what we believe

What I truly believe about God is not simply what I say. It is not what I recite. What I truly believe about God is seen in how I live. It is seen in the way that I treat people, what I do with my money, how I handle those with whom I disagree. It is reflected in what I give my time, my energy and my attention to. Too often, we allow ourselves to

16   NOVAK, Michael, *Belief & Unbelief: A Philosophy Of Self-Knowledge* (Piscataway, NJ: Transaction Publishers, 1994).
17   See Matthew 2, particularly v. 8.
18   See 2 Samuel 11.
19   See James 2:14-26, NB v. 17.
20   Margaret Thatcher was played by Meryl Streep in The Iron Lady released in 2011 by Pathé, Film 2, The UK Film Council, The Weinstein Company, Yuk Films, Canal+, CineCinema, Goldcrest Films and DJ Films. It was distributed by Pathé International and 20th Century Fox. It was written by Abi Morgan and directed by Phyllida Lloyd.

be lulled into the idea that if we say something we believe it. That just isn't true. The truth is that if we believe something, then we will live it and in order to reinforce what we believe we must live it out, even when we do not feel like it.

As uncomfortable as it might be, our churches, our Christian communities, reflect what we actually *believe* about God. They demonstrate our priorities, our values and our convictions. If we want to know what we believe about God, then we need to look at the way we behave and the way our *churches* behave.

That might prove to be a little distressing for many of us, but it is an important principle. Yet at the same time, we all know the struggle and the pain, and perhaps the personal dilemma, of actually doing things we don't want to do! Like the Apostle Paul,[21] we find ourselves absolutely committed to something in our heads, hearts and intentions, but not always following it through in our decisions, attitudes and actions. It would appear that we can, sometimes, believe something yet at the same time not appear to believe it. There are lots of reasons for that apparent paradox.

The cry of the conflicted - 'I believe, help my unbelief'

What does my faith say about the pain of the world?

Many things cause us to struggle with our faith. Hardship, disappointment, and unanswered prayer are just a few. Our questions can drown out God's voice. Why didn't he heal my dad? Why did he let the Boxing Day Tsunami take 250,000 lives? Why does God seem so distant and uncaring? How do we believe in the face of such suffering?

What does my faith say about the controversies in the Church?

We can also struggle because we hear voices from within the Church around us that seem to be challenging, or even undermining, what we thought were core convictions of Christianity. Internal voices in the Church can undermine our faith and convictions by questioning some of the things that we thought were certainties. From the Virgin Birth to the Resurrection, from the uniqueness of Christ to what happens to us when we die, all around us there are Christian voices with conflicting ideas. How do we believe in the midst of such virulent debate?

What does my faith say about the competing claims to truth?

There are many voices around us today that question the validity of Christianity. How can we believe in Jesus as the unique and only way for a valid relationship with God when we live alongside people of other faiths? Aren't we being arrogant? Surely 'Allah' and 'Yahweh' are the same, really? Why can't Jesus be one of a number of options for people? Won't God welcome all 'good people'?

---

21   See Romans 6 and 7 in particular.

Unbelievable confidence

There is a remarkable story recounted in Mark's Gospel about a man whose son was possessed by a demonic spirit. You'll find it in Mark 9:14-29:

When they came to the disciples, they saw a great crowd around them, and some scribes arguing with them. When the whole crowd saw him, they were immediately overcome with awe, and they ran forward to greet him. He asked them, "What are you arguing about with them?" Someone from the crowd answered him, "Teacher, I brought you my son; he has a spirit that makes him unable to speak; and whenever it seizes him, it dashes him down; and he foams and grinds his teeth and becomes rigid; and I asked your disciples to cast it out, but they could not do so." He answered them, "You faithless generation, how much longer must I be among you? How much longer must I put up with you? Bring him to me." And they brought the boy to him. When the spirit saw him, immediately it convulsed the boy, and he fell on the ground and rolled about, foaming at the mouth. Jesus asked the father, "How long has this been happening to him?" And he said, "From childhood. It has often cast him into the fire and into the water, to destroy him; but if you are able to do anything, have pity on us and help us." Jesus said to him, "If you are able! — All things can be done for the one who believes." Immediately the father of the child cried out, "I believe; help my unbelief!" When Jesus saw that a crowd came running together, he rebuked the unclean spirit, saying to it, "You spirit that keeps this boy from speaking and hearing, I command you, come out of him, and never enter him again!" After crying out and convulsing him terribly, it came out, and the boy was like a corpse, so that most of them said, "He is dead." But Jesus took him by the hand and lifted him up, and he was able to stand. When he had entered the house, his disciples asked him privately, "Why could we not cast it out?" He said to them, "This kind can come out only through prayer."
Mark 9:14-29 (NIV)

The story is one of desperation. This father, like any good father, would do anything to save his son. He has tried everything else, so he brings the boy to Jesus. His faith is not strong, but he comes anyway. Jesus' disciples hadn't helped (v18) and the father is running out of options. So he finds himself before Jesus with his son. You can hear the desperation in his voice:

IF YOU ARE ABLE TO DO ANYTHING, HAVE PITY ON US AND HELP US.
(Verse 22)

Jesus' reply to the man is swift. He almost sounds offended by the father's use of the word 'if' (see verse 23). Yet Jesus tells the man that faith is a powerful thing:

ALL THINGS CAN BE DONE FOR THE ONE WHO BELIEVES.
(Verse 23)

So the desperate father cries out to Jesus:

I BELIEVE, HELP MY UNBELIEF!
(Verse 24)

Despite the fact that this father has been disappointed by Jesus' disciples; despite the fact that Jesus has not done anything to help the young demon-possessed boy yet; despite his own deep struggles as a father, this man cries out to God with the faith that he has. Jesus delivers the boy of the demon but the boy then seems to die. Jesus then takes the boy by the hand and raises him to life again.

This father came with a shaky faith, an uncertain hope and a deep yearning in his heart, and God met him. His cry, "I believe, help my unbelief", is familiar to anyone who has felt the conflicting grip of doubt and despair whilst holding on to belief in a God who is good and whose mercy endures forever. That father's statement is the inspiration behind *Unbelievable*.

• *Unbelievable* is birthed out of a desire to help us to connect what we believe to how we live. Despite all the changes that the Church is going through and all the challenges that the Church faces, it is still possible to have confidence in God and his purposes in the world.

• *Unbelievable* springs out of the conviction that God has revealed himself uniquely and centrally to us through his Son, the Lord Jesus Christ. It is rooted in the belief that God has given us a faithful and accurate account of his dealings with the world and his purpose on the planet through the collection of books we call the Bible.

• *Unbelievable* is rooted in the conviction that the great Creeds of the church capture the truths of scripture and unite Christians everywhere in reliable, shaping and solid truth that can set us free from the double dangers of relativism (being absorbed into our culture) and exclusivism (running away from our culture).

• *Unbelievable* flows in the stream that celebrates the present power of the Holy Spirit and seeks not only to *learn about* God but also to *encounter him*.

We've a lot to be confident about

THOUGH AN ARMY ENCAMPS AGAINST ME, MY HEART SHALL NOT FEAR; THOUGH WAR RISE UP AGAINST ME, YET I WILL BE CONFIDENT.

Psalm 27:3 (NRSV)

In the midst of all the uncertainties of life and the unpredictability of events around us, we can be confident that God is good and that his love endures forever. We don't have to pretend to have all the answers; we can be honest about our questions, open about our struggles and humble enough to admit our own faults and failings. God is strong enough to cope with our uncertainties. He doesn't expect us to be perfect, he expects us to be honest.

Unbreakable... Unbelievable

Josh and Sophie, who were brother and sister, were playing in their living room. They had built a tent and as they crouched inside, they had invented their own little world. It was full of adventurers and pirates and heroes. To build the tent, they had held one corner of a sheet secure on the mantelpiece by placing an old, heavy ornament on top of it- but they were careful not to move the ornament in case it broke. They were always conscious of not wanting to break the ornament, but as the afternoon progressed they began to enjoy the game. At the same time, they began to forget about the ornament.

As they were swaying on the open sea and Josh was defending Sophie from the ferocious pirate that had just boarded the ship, Josh jumped up in the air with his wooden sword. As he did, the sheet lifted high above his head! Josh and Sophie saw the ornament on the corner of the mantelpiece fly up into the air. They winced as they waited for terrible noise of it hitting the hearth and breaking into tiny pieces. They knew they were going to be in so much trouble! Instead of the ornament breaking, however, it bounced along the hearth and came to a halt at the feet of their mum, who had heard the bang and walked into the living room. She bent down and picked up the ornament and looked at Josh and Sophie.

"Good job this is unbreakable!" she said, smiling. She set the ornament back onto the mantelpiece and told the children to be careful.

Josh looked at Sophie, his young eyes wide with wonder. "It's unbreakable, Sophie," he gasped, "if we had known that in the first place, think of the fun we might have had!"

Sophie smiled back, "It's unbreakable, Josh – how unbelievable is that?!"

Unfathomable... Unbeatable...Unstoppable

Christian faith is unbreakable. It is not a porcelain figurine made to be handled fearfully and tentatively. It is unbreakable. It is robust. It can face the challenges of our culture, the anxieties of our heart and the questions of our sorrows and doubts. This faith changes us. It transforms and renews us because at its centre there is a Father who is unfathomable, a Son who is unbeatable and a Spirit who is unstoppable.

The Theme Guide will help us to see this God again, to rejoice in who he is, what he wants to do in the world through us and what he wants to do in us.

God has not finished with you yet. He hasn't finished with his Church yet, and he hasn't finished with the world yet. The best is yet to be.

Unbelievable.

Lord,
I have held you like a porcelain figurine.
I have been fearful that the slightest knock to what
I believe will crack my trust in you.
I have sought to defend you when you want to
defend me.
I've found myself running from the world,
hiding away from the reality of life
And using my faith as a shelter from living.
I don't want to be like that anymore.

Unbreakable God,
Help me to discover how much
you are committed to me.
Give me fresh confidence
to step into my life
day by day knowing that
You are Unbreakable.
You are Unchanging.
You are more committed to me than I am to you.
Come and meet me in the honesty of this moment,
reveal to me again your wonder and your grace
And let me step into a new adventure of faith and
life with you.

Amen.

You can read more about how what we think
shapes what we become in section one of the
Theme Book – *Unbelievable: Confident Faith In A
Sceptical World* by Malcolm Duncan.

The morning Bible studies will also help you to think
through what you really believe as they explore
the truths behind The Apostles' Creed.

WHAT WE BELIEVE:
Why the Apostles' Creed?

I BELIEVE IN GOD, THE FATHER ALMIGHTY, CREATOR OF HEAVEN AND EARTH. I BELIEVE IN JESUS CHRIST, HIS ONLY SON, OUR LORD. HE WAS CONCEIVED BY THE POWER OF THE HOLY SPIRIT AND BORN OF THE VIRGIN MARY. HE SUFFERED UNDER PONTIUS PILATE, WAS CRUCIFIED, DIED, AND WAS BURIED. HE DESCENDED TO THE DEAD. ON THE THIRD DAY HE ROSE AGAIN. HE ASCENDED INTO HEAVEN, AND IS SEATED AT THE RIGHT HAND OF THE FATHER. HE WILL COME AGAIN TO JUDGE THE LIVING AND THE DEAD. I BELIEVE IN THE HOLY SPIRIT, THE HOLY CATHOLIC CHURCH, THE COMMUNION OF SAINTS, THE FORGIVENESS OF SINS, THE RESURRECTION OF THE BODY, AND THE LIFE EVERLASTING. AMEN.

A creed that unites us

If you are a follower of Jesus Christ then you are one of around two billion Christians in the world today.[22] That's just under one third of the world's population. There were around 1,600 Christian streams and denominations in the world in the year 1900. Today, there are somewhere between 21,000 and 34,000![23] There are, however, just 5 major blocks of Christian belief today. These are (listed alphabetically):

- **Anglicans (around 70.5 million people)**
- **Independents (around 275.5 million people)**
- **Other Protestants (around 400 million people)**
- **Orthodox (around 218 million people)**
- **Roman Catholics (around 1 billion people)**

---

22   You can find out more at www.religioustolerance.org.
23   See BARRETT, David A., World Christian Encyclopedia (Oxford University Press, 1982) which estimates almost 21,000 denominations, and the updated World Christian Encyclopedia (BARRETT et. al, Oxford University Press, 2nd edition, 2001) which estimates at least 33,000. 'Denomination' is defined as "an organised Christian group within a country". For further information, see The Center for the Study of Global Christianity at Gordon-Conwell Theological Seminary which estimated 34,000 denominations in 2000, rising to an estimated 43,000 in 2012. There is general agreement that there were around 1,600 recognizable Christian denominations around the year 1900

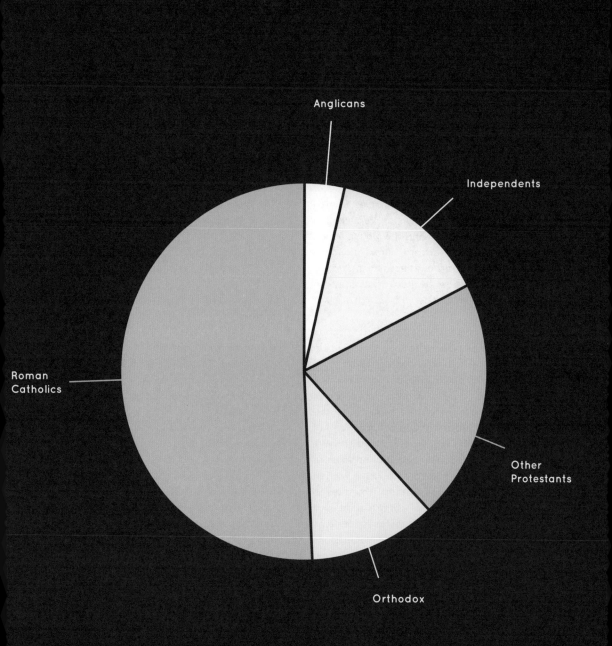

Anglicans

Independents

Roman
Catholics

Other
Protestants

Orthodox

There are many things that divide us. From the rite of baptism to the way we celebrate the meal that remembers the death of Jesus and how we handle the Bible, there are a lot of different views and conflicting ideas. We have different views of the roles of priests and pastors, the roles of men and women, the place and form of worship and music in the life of a church and the way in which we make decisions and govern ourselves. Many of these divisions are an embarrassment to the Church and a bad witness to the world, but some of them are helpful and good.

Yet every single major Christian denomination and stream in the world today is united in its acceptance of the Apostles' Creed.[24] This statement of belief and confession of what we, as Christians, hold to be central to our faith was first mentioned in a letter written by Ambrose, the Bishop of Milan, in 390 A.D. If you are from one of the more established traditions of Christianity, then you may well have been encouraged to learn it so that you could repeat it off by heart. It is often used in Anglican and Roman Catholic churches to prepare people for the rite of confirmation, and in most of the established Protestant traditions of Christianity it is affirmed in early confessions and catechisms that were (and are) used to help Christians understand what we truly believe.

Many of us may not know very much about the Apostles' Creed. We may even wonder why it is important to affirm it. What does it matter? Well, it matters for lots of reasons – here are just a few:

- The Apostles' Creed has united Christians for somewhere in the region of 1750 years;

- It cuts through many of the 'non-vital' issues and focuses on the heart of the matter;

- It affirms great truths that hold us in the midst of great controversies and challenges;

- It is thoroughly rooted in the books and letters of the New Testament, and probably captures the teaching and convictions of the early Church in a way that can be remembered;

- It is a 'living confession' that is still used by the vast majority of Jesus' followers around the world;

- It is a statement of BELIEF and of FAITH, not just words that we recite, but truths that change us and shape us;

- The Apostles' Creed gives us confidence and reminds us that we are part of the Church around the world, not just one small section of it;

- It reminds us of the greatness of God and of what he has done to redeem and transform us and the world in which we live.

---

24   There are, in fact, five 'early creeds'. They are the Apostles' Creed (emerging between 200 A.D. and c450 A.D.); the Nicene Creed (325 A.D.) and the related Nicene-Constantinopolitan Creed (382 A.D.); the Chalcedonian Creed (sometimes called the Chalcedonian Principle or the Chalcedonian Declaration, 451 A.D.); and the Athanasian Creed (500 A.D.).

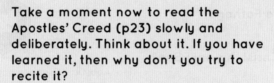

Take a moment now to read the Apostles' Creed (p23) slowly and deliberately. Think about it. If you have learned it, then why don't you try to recite it?

Do you really believe in these truths? What impact do they have on the way you view the world, yourself and your place in it?

The Apostles' Creed and Unbelievable.

Unbelievable is rooted in the Apostles' Creed. Each morning, our Bible teachers will be exploring the Creed phrase by phrase. They'll be teaching the great biblical truths that lie behind the Creed and helping us to see the ways in which confidence in what we believe can translate into confidence in how we live.

To help us understand the biblical truth behind the Creed, our Bible teachers will look at the Apostles' Creed through the lenses of three core statements at the heart of it:

- **I believe in God, the Father Almighty...**

- **I believe in Jesus Christ, his only Son, our Lord...**

- **I believe in the Holy Spirit...**

By looking at this ancient creedal confession, we will be rooting ourselves in the truths of scripture about God and his purposes in the world. We'll discover again that God has a purpose and a plan for his people, his church and the world. As we take a few days to stop and think about the great truths at the heart of Christian faith, we will discover that it is possible to face a world of uncertainty with confidence without sounding arrogant. As we focus on God, we'll find the attention shifting from us to him. When that begins to happen, confidence begins to rise in us because we realise that God has not finished with us yet.

The Apostles' Creed is not just a set of words that you learn and speak out loud. They are truths that we declare – to ourselves, to one another in the church and to the world. They hold us together – in more ways than one. The word 'creed' is based on the Latin verb '*credo*' that means 'I believe'. Take a few moments to reflect on the words of Matthew 6 from *The Message*, shown here and ask God to help you shift your focus from yourself to him this week. So often we come away to things like Spring Harvest and we ask God to change the circumstances at home. What if God wants to change you, though? What if he wants to do a work in you so that you can face the same circumstances with a new-found confidence and faith?

Here's what I want you to do: Find a quiet, secluded place so you won't be tempted to role-play before God. Just be there as simply and honestly as you can manage. The focus will shift from you to God, and you will begin to sense his grace.
Matthew 6:6 (The Message)

The recordings of the Bible studies each morning will help you to dig into the Apostles' Creed more deeply and will enable you to understand how the rest of the material at this year's Spring Harvest fits together. Don't worry if you cannot get to the Bible studies in the Big Top, though, as the rest of the day will still make sense and connect together. Don't forget you can order the recordings of the Bible studies, or attend the second session of the Bible studies, where you will be able to benefit from the teaching and the discussion that flows out of them.

OUR CONFIDENCE IN GOD

DO NOT LET YOUR HEARTS BE TROUBLED. BELIEVE IN GOD, BELIEVE ALSO IN ME.

John 14:1 (NRSV)

GOD IS A SAFE PLACE TO HIDE,
READY TO HELP WHEN WE NEED HIM.
WE STAND FEARLESS AT THE CLIFF EDGE OF DOOM,
COURAGEOUS IN SEASTORM AND EARTHQUAKE,
BEFORE THE RUSH AND ROAR OF OCEANS,
THE TREMORS THAT SHIFT MOUNTAINS.

JACOB-WRESTLING GOD FIGHTS FOR US,
GOD OF THE ANGEL ARMIES PROTECTS US.

Psalm 46:1-3 (The Message)

FAITH IS A LIVING,
DARING CONFIDENCE IN GOD'S GRACE,
SO SURE AND CERTAIN
THAT A MAN COULD STAKE HIS LIFE
ON IT A THOUSAND TIMES.

Martin Luther

The Spring Harvest theme this year is deeply rooted in God and his character. He is trustworthy, dependable and faithful. We cannot manipulate him, change him or diminish him, and that is precisely why we can have confidence in him. Our confidence is not based on our strength, but his. We are not confident because we are strong, but because he is. We do not gain our confidence from the fact that society agrees with us or even approves of us. Our confidence comes from the fact that God is true to his word and utterly committed to his people (individually and collectively) and utterly committed to his purposes in the world.

A person's last words can tell us a great deal about their priorities and their convictions. On the night before Jesus was murdered, he told his disciples that they could have confidence in him and confidence in his Father, despite what was about to happen and what they were about to go through. Jesus told them to keep trusting despite the massive changes they were going to experience. God could be trusted in the midst of great change. He still can be.

"The colours of the world are changing, day by day," Enjolras sings in a famous line from the musical *Les Miserables*, based on the book of the same name by Victor Hugo. He's right! If you stop and think about it for a moment, there is a lot changing in the world – there always has been. Yet he is the same as he has always been and because of that, we can trust him.

Just look across the last ten years of your life and you will see change on every front. Technology advancing faster and faster with new ways of seeing one another, speaking to one another and communicating with one another. In the UK, we spend around nine hours a day in front of screens (that's about 30 years of your life)! We email, text, tweet, Skype, Facebook and Facetime. Forty percent of adults use a smartphone in the UK. We send well in excess of 220 million texts a day. In the UK, we text more than we talk![25]

It feels like change is all around us. In the last ten years, as a nation we have seen significant changes in our demographics, our religious outlook, our politics and the way we understand the family and its purpose. The figures from the 2011 census show that whilst Christianity is still the largest 'religion' in the UK almost 25% of the population describe themselves as having no religion at all.[26]

---

25   See 'UK is now texting more than talking' accessed in October 2012 at http://media.ofcom.org.uk/2012/07/18/uk-is-now-texting-more-than-talking.
26   See Religion In England And Wales, published by the Office for National Statistics. Further information available at www.ons.gov.uk.

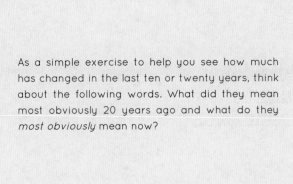

As a simple exercise to help you see how much has changed in the last ten or twenty years, think about the following words. What did they mean most obviously 20 years ago and what do they *most obviously* mean now?

Word	What it *most obviously* meant in 1994	What it *most obviously* means in 2014
Web		
Twitter		
Outlook		
Powerpoint		
Tablet		
Orange		
Blackberry		

Changes in Religious Affiliation in the UK between 2001 and 2011 [27]

Number of People	Percentage of the Population	Religious Affiliation	Change since the last census in 2001
33.2 million	59.3%	Christianity	A decrease from 71.7%. (This equates to a decline of 17% in overall numbers of self-confessing Christians.)
2.7 million	4.8%	Muslim	An increase from 3%. (This equates to an increase of 60% in overall numbers of self-confessing Muslims.)
14.1 million	25.1%	No religious affiliation at all	An increase of 10.3%. (This equates to an increase of 59% in overall numbers of those who self-identify as not having any religious affiliation at all.)

27   ibid.

Lessons from King Cnut Change is here to stay: learning to respond with confidence rather than react with anger

King Cnut was a Danish King who reigned in England from 1016-1035. Cnut's father was the first Christianised King of Denmark and religious zeal became an important part of the family's dynasty. In fact, much of Cnut's reign in England was characterized by his attempts to force faith onto others and to manipulate the power bases around him because of his apparent faith. The most famous story about Cnut is his failed attempt to command the sea to stop rising. The story is found in the twelfth century *Chronicle* recorded by Henry of Huntingdon. Although it is often quoted to tell of Cnut's pride, when you actually read what Henry wrote, you realize that Cnut makes a powerful declaration that acknowledges his own weakness and Christ's great strength:

With the greatest vigour he commanded that his chair should be set on the shore, when the tide began to rise. And then he spoke to the rising sea saying "You are part of my dominion, and the ground that I am seated upon is mine, nor has anyone disobeyed my orders with impunity. Therefore, I order you not to rise onto my land, nor to wet the clothes or body of your Lord". But the sea carried on rising as usual without any reverence for his person, and soaked his feet and legs. Then he moving away said: "All the inhabitants of the world should know that the power of kings is vain and trivial, and that none is worthy of the name of king but He whose command the heaven, earth and sea obey by eternal laws". Therefore King Cnut never afterwards placed the crown on his head, but above a picture of the Lord nailed to the cross, turning it forever into a means to praise God, the great king. By whose mercy may the soul of King Cnut enjoy peace.
Henry of Huntingdon, *Chronicle*[28]

We can't avoid change. If we try to, we will end up sounding angry and driven by reactions rather than sounding Christ-like and responding to the world around us. King Cnut was an 11th century King of England who has become famous for his alleged arrogance in commanding the sea to stop rising. Yet, when you read the actual account of the event that gave birth to this story, you realise that whilst his initial assumption was definitely arrogant, King Cnut quickly realised his mistake in assuming that he was in control of everything, and from the moment he acknowledged that he could not command the sea, he placed his own crown above a picture of the Lord Jesus, whom he saw as the Great King.

28   FORESTER, Thomas, ed. and tr., The Chronicle Of Henry Of Huntingdon. Comprising The History Of England, From The Invasion Of Julius Cæsar To The Accession Of Henry II. Also, The Acts Of Stephen, king Of England And Duke of Normandy, (London: H.G. Bohn, 1853).

Our powerlessness doesn't need to mean helplessness or despair

The world around us is changing – and not always for the better. We are not faced with the decision to change with it or become irrelevant, though. Although the world is changing, God remains faithful, reliable, strong and dependable. His word can still be trusted. As the children of Israel repeated again and again, God is still good and his love endures forever.[29] His goodness is not determined by what is happening around us, in us or in the world. Instead, his goodness is determined by his character and what he has shown us about himself.

Sometimes we are confronted with the *wrong* options when it comes to coping with the changes taking place around us. We don't have to end up sounding like an angry mob shouting at the world because we don't like what it is doing, nor do we have to just accept everything that is happening around us as if we can't change anything. What if we remain true to our convictions and continue to stand up for what we believe in, but we do so with confidence that God is good and that he is with us? We don't have to allow what we see in the world to dictate what we believe about God, do we? What if we allow what we believe about God to shape the way we view the world? Isn't that a better way of looking at it?

There are plenty of examples of Christians who allowed what they believed about God to shape the way they viewed the world. Believing in God and having confidence in him can change the way you view the rest of the world. Too often, our confidence rests in believing that God will do what *we want*. That is not confidence, though – that is presumption. Our confidence should lie in the belief that God will do *what he wants* and what he wants is always right – even when we do not understand it. We do not have to understand God to trust him, but if we are to have any understanding of him at all, then we do need to trust him.

> I BELIEVE IN CHRISTIANITY AS I BELIEVE THAT THE SUN HAS RISEN: NOT ONLY BECAUSE I SEE IT, BUT BECAUSE BY IT I SEE EVERYTHING ELSE.
>
> C.S. Lewis, *The Weight of Glory*[30]

> I AM THE LORD, AND I DO NOT CHANGE. THAT IS WHY YOU…ARE NOT ALREADY DESTROYED. EVER SINCE THE DAYS OF YOUR ANCESTORS, YOU HAVE SCORNED MY DECREES AND FAILED TO OBEY THEM. NOW RETURN TO ME, AND I WILL RETURN TO YOU, SAYS THE LORD OF HEAVEN'S ARMIES.
>
> Malachi 3:6-7 (NLT)

> HEAVEN AND EARTH WILL PASS AWAY, BUT MY WORDS WILL NOT PASS AWAY.
>
> Matthew 24:35 (NRSV)

---

29   For example, see Psalm 34, 100, 118, 135, 136, 138, 145. See also 2 Samuel 7; 1 Chronicles 17, Jeremiah 33, Lamentations 3, Nahum 1 and 1 Peter 2.

30   LEWIS, C.S., The Weight of Glory and Other Addresses (London: S.P.C.K., 1949).

Trust God from the bottom of your heart;
Don't try to figure out everything on your own.
Listen for God's voice in everything you do,
everywhere you go;
he's the one who will keep you on track.
Don't assume that you know it all.
Run to God! Run from evil!
Your body will glow with health,
your very bones will vibrate with life!
Honour God with everything you own;
give him the first and the best.
Your barns will burst,
your wine vats will brim over.
But don't, dear friend, resent God's discipline;
don't sulk under his loving correction.
It's the child he loves that God corrects;
a father's delight is behind all this.
Proverbs 3:5-12 (The Message)

Reinhold Niebuhr was probably one of the USA's most influential theologians in the 20th century. Political leaders such as Barack Obama, Jimmy Carter, Hilary Rodham Clinton, Martin Luther King Jr., Madeleine Albright and John McCain have all claimed to be heavily influenced by him. He is probably most popularly known for writing what is now called The Serenity Prayer. Take time to pray through it slowly. What are the things that you cannot change, what are the things you can change, and how does the utter reliability of God help you to face them? The second half of the prayer is often overlooked – but it contains a deep acknowledgment of the grace and the reliability of God for us.

God grant me the serenity
to accept the things I cannot change;
courage to change the things I can;
and wisdom to know the difference.
Living one day at a time;
enjoying one moment at a time;
accepting hardships as the pathway to peace;
taking, as he did, this sinful world
as it is, not as I would have it;
trusting that he will make all things right
if I surrender to his Will;
that I may be reasonably happy in this life
and supremely happy with him
Forever in the next.
Amen.

The Unfathomable Father

The Big Start
The Father we
can trust

Celebrations
The Father we
long for

**The
Unfathomable
Father**

"Now we call him,
Abba, Father"
Romans 8:15 (NLT)

Bible Study
"I believe in God, the
Father Almighty,
Creator of heaven
and earth."

**Spaces and
Seminars**
The God who made
us knows us. He is both
powerful and
personal

THE FATHER WE CAN TRUST

This morning in the Big Start we'll be exploring the fact that we can trust God because he is both our Father and he is good. There are many times that we can forget this, but the reality at the heart of Christianity is that God is a loving Father who will not abandon his children. We'll be exploring the wonderful story in Luke 11:9-13, so why not read this passage this morning before you join the Big Start and think about the ways in which God is a good Father to you and your family.

And so I tell you, keep on asking, and you will receive what you ask for. Keep on seeking, and you will find. Keep on knocking, and the door will be opened to you. For everyone who asks, receives. Everyone who seeks, finds. And to everyone who knocks, the door will be opened. You fathers—if your children ask for a fish, do you give them a snake instead? Or if they ask for an egg, do you give them a scorpion? Of course not! So if you sinful people know how to give good gifts to your children, how much more will your heavenly Father give the Holy Spirit to those who ask him.
Luke 11:9-13 (NLT)

Don't just think about the Father, talk to him

The comedian Dawn French once said:

> IT WAS MY FATHER WHO TAUGHT ME TO VALUE MYSELF. HE TOLD ME THAT I WAS UNCOMMONLY BEAUTIFUL AND THAT I WAS THE MOST PRECIOUS THING IN HIS LIFE.
>
> Dawn French[31]

Many people have had wonderful relationships with their fathers and many people have not. God promises to be a good father to his children. Take a few moments during the day to thank God for his kindness and his father heart toward you. Perhaps you can do that by praying the most famous prayer in the Christian tradition – The Lord's Prayer. Remember again that it all springs from God's 'fatherhood' of us. Use whichever version you are least familiar with to help you to discover new depth in this wonderful prayer. Why not try writing your own interpretation of The Lord's Prayer?

> TO BE A CHRISTIAN WITHOUT PRAYER IS NO MORE POSSIBLE THAN TO BE ALIVE WITHOUT BREATHING.
>
> Martin Luther (1483 – 1546)

---

31   FRENCH, Dawn, Dear Fatty (London: Arrow Books, 2009).

Our Father in heaven, hallowed be your name,
your kingdom come, your will be done,
on earth as it is in heaven.
Give us today our daily bread.
And forgive us our debts,
as we also have forgiven our debtors.
And lead us not into temptation,
but deliver us from the evil one.
Matthew 6:9-13 (NIV)

Our Father in heaven, may your name be kept holy.
May your Kingdom come soon.
May your will be done on earth, as it is in heaven.
Give us today the food we need,
and forgive us our sins,
as we have forgiven those who sin against us.
And don't let us yield to temptation,
but rescue us from the evil one.
Matthew 6:9-13 (NLT)

Our Father in heaven, reveal who you are.
Set the world right;
Do what's best—as above, so below.
Keep us alive with three square meals.
Keep us forgiven with you and forgiving others.
Keep us safe from ourselves and the Devil.
You're in charge!
You can do anything you want!
You're ablaze in beauty!
Yes. Yes. Yes.
Matthew 6:9-13 (The Message)

Our Father who is in heaven,
hallowed (kept holy) be your name.
your kingdom come,
your will be done on earth as it is in heaven.
Give us this day our daily bread.
And forgive us our debts, as we also have forgiven
(left, remitted, and let go of the debts,
and have given up resentment against) our debtors.
And lead (bring) us not into temptation,
but deliver us from the evil one.
For yours is the kingdom
and the power and the glory forever.
Amen.
Matthew 6:9-13 (Amplified Bible)

WE BELIEVE IN GOD THE FATHER ALMIGHTY

The Bible study today will explore the first statement of the Apostles' Creed[32]:

I BELIEVE IN GOD, THE FATHER ALMIGHTY, CREATOR OF HEAVEN AND EARTH.

It is simply impossible to begin to understand Christianity without first grasping the importance of the profound truth that God is our father. Without this foundation at the heart of our faith, we are likely to fall into a trembling fear of God, always trying to please him and never succeeding. It is, perhaps, the most profound truth in the Christian faith that God is approachable. That he is our Creator and our Sustainer.

Without this heartbeat, our spiritual lives will become monotonous and lifeless, or we will be driven by the constant need to seek God's approval or win his favour.

The Hebrew idea of 'believing' is not simply a mental assent to a set of statements, it is the commitment to build your whole life around the reality that you claim is at the heart of your convictions.

As the Bible study explores the heart of 'God, the Father Almighty, Creator of heaven and earth' we will discover not only God's fatherhood of *us personally* but also his fatherhood of the *whole creation*. Perhaps now, more than at any other time in history, the idea of God as the Father and Sustainer of the whole planet needs to be discovered again and allowed to shape the way we engage with the environment and the created world.

---

32   The fatherhood of God can be explored in Scriptures such as Genesis 1-3; Isaiah 9:6; Hosea 11; Romans 8:14-17 and Colossians 1:1-23.

The goodness of the Father

I have been privileged to stand in jaw-dropped amazement in several places in recent years – in intensely spiritual moments, my whole being cried out in exultation – whilst maintaining an entirely cool exterior, of course! Well, almost.

The cable car to Klein Matterhorn carries over a hundred people out over the glacier, the weight causing the cable to sag. The air is thin, crisp and cold. The Matterhorn, well over 4000m, dominates the scene. Everything is 'Wow'! Eventually the car climbs up towards Klein and a distant Alp appears.

It is even more amazingly beautiful. Then the car rises up above the ridge and a cry comes from everyone in the car as more peaks than you can count suddenly appear. God reminds me - his creativity is boundless...

I stood a few feet from the edge of Niagara Falls – where water from half a continent falls away. Mists swirl, and it's impossible to comprehend that amount of water. I feel God saying "This extravagance proclaims my power and might". I pause, then read the noticeboard. It informs me that nowadays, only 10% of the water flows over the Falls – the rest is used for Hydro power. God reminds me he is much bigger than I can even begin to understand...

David Dorricott
Trustee of Spring Harvest Holidays
and Memralife Group

THE GOD WHO MADE US KNOWS US

Father-hunger

"I gave a directed retreat recently to a very fine man, a priest who has driven himself to be perfect, successful. We were trying to determine where that drive was coming from. A great silence ensued that was almost embarrassing and I could see that something was happening," recalls Father Richard Rohr, O.F.M., an internationally known retreat director, author and lecturer.

"'It's like a chasm. It's like a canyon,' the priest said.

"'What is?' I asked.

"'The depth of the emptiness and pain of my relationship with my father,' he replied. All he could keep saying was, 'It's like a canyon.'

"Here was a man who looked very productive and creative. And he was, but in his 40's his world started collapsing because he was always driven by a need to please his father. Nothing he ever did for his father was right. He transferred that need to please the Church, the bishop and the people. But that drive was keeping him from the real experience that he already was loved by God.

"That little example is the story of much of the Church as far as I am concerned. This father hunger is running so many things for good and for ill. When we don't recognize we are seeking love and approval from the absent father, then we become compulsive, frenetic, busy, wild in a bad sense. That is why we need power, sex and money. We don't recognize that what is really at work is father hunger.

"I find this father wound to be even bigger and deeper than I first had expected years ago. There is a father hunger in society that is unrecognized, unnamed, not seen as that. It is seen in the people who rage toward society, and in the need for authority – for someone else to tell them what to do. Underneath all of that there is a father wound out of which comes a tremendous father hunger in our society that is showing its face in so, so many ways." [33]

---

33   'Naming the Father Hunger: An interview with Richard Rohr'.
Available at http://www.malespirituality.org/father_hunger.htm. Accessed 26 July 2013.

What does it mean to believe in God the Father?

One of the greatest privileges of life is parenting. To be afforded the honour of being a mother or a father should never be taken for granted. Yet so often we get it wrong! Stories such as those of Constance Briscoe[34] or Dave Pelzer[35] tell us, in graphic detail, of the consequences of bad parenting. It can be a difficult thing to think about God as your Father when you have had a bad experience of fatherhood in your life. Yet it can also be releasing and life-giving to discover the kind of Father that God actually is.

We run three risks when we think about God as our 'Father'. The first is to avoid the idea all together, because we have had a bad experience. The second is to over-sentimentalise the idea and turn it into nothing more than a nice fluffy feeling. The third is to take the idea of Father and super-impose a 21st century concept of fatherhood onto God. We need to avoid all three pitfalls and think of ways of stopping ourselves from making God a big version of ourselves or a construct of our innermost desires.

In his book, *The Forgotten Father*, Tom Smail wrote:

I NEVER KNEW MY FATHER. HE DIED WHEN I WAS TOO YOUNG TO REALIZE WHAT I HAD LOST. BUT I HAVE BEEN DISCOVERING SLOWLY EVER SINCE. WE ARE ALL SHAPED BY OUR LACKS AS MUCH AS BY OUR GIFTS, FOR NONE OF US STARTS COMPLETE.

Tom Smail, The Forgotten Father[36]

Is Smail right? Could it possibly be true that without a true understanding of God as a Father, we cannot understand the heart of the Gospel, as the title of his book suggests? If you think about it, not only could Tom Smail be right, he must be right because if we have a wrong understanding of who God is then everything else in our relationship with him will be coloured and impacted by this primary observation. "I believe in God, the Father Almighty, Creator of heaven and earth," is a declaration of first principles that shapes almost all of the rest of our understanding of God, his relationship with us and our place in the world. This declaration articulates several important principles:

- God the Father – God is personal, knowable and has communicated his character with us.

- Almighty – God is powerful and strong and dependable.

- Creator of heaven and earth – God is purposeful. He has created the world and everything in it and has a clear and intentional plan.

---

34 BRISCOE, Constance, Ugly (London: Hodder, 2006).
35 PELZER, Dave, A Child Called It: One Child's Courage To Survive (London: Orion, 1995).
36 SMAIL, Tom, The Forgotten Father: Rediscovering The Heart Of The Christian Gospel (London: Paternoster Press, 1996).

God the Father is personal

Throughout the history of Christianity, we have had no hesitation in speaking of God in personal terms. We ascribe a whole series of 'personal' attributes to God such as 'love' and 'purpose'. The Christian understanding of prayer is largely modelled on the relationship between a child and a parent. The idea of 'reconciliation', so central to Paul's understanding of salvation itself, is based on a broken personal relationship being restored.

We need to be careful though. Just because God is 'personal' doesn't mean we can make him a human being! God is not, in the words of Paul Tillich, located just in one place, for example. Not only that, but Christianity believes in God as 'One but Three'. God exists as Father, Son and Holy Spirit. When we say we believe in God as a 'person', then, we are not suggesting that he is limited to our human understanding of personhood. He is not limited by lack of knowledge, he is not limited by having to be in only one place at once, and he is not limited by lack of power. As we explore the idea of God the Father as a personal God we need to start with the way he is viewed in the Bible.

A pathway into clarity – the journey from the Old to the New Testament

The Old Testament

The New Testament concept of *God as Father* is profoundly clearer than the pictures of God as Father in the Old Testament. It is almost like the Old Testament contains shadows of the idea, with God appearing as the Father of Israel[37] or the Father of certain individuals.[38] Sometimes, the idea or the 'rumour' of God as a father is present in the Old Testament even if the word 'father' itself is absent.[39]

It is interesting to reflect on some of the passages from the Old Testament that paint the picture of God's 'fatherhood':

Yet, O Lord, you are our Father; we are the clay, and you are our potter; we are all the work of your hand. Do not be exceedingly angry, O Lord, and do not remember iniquity forever.
Isaiah 64: 8-9 (NRSV)

---

37   See Deuteronomy 32:6; Isaiah 63:16; 64:8; Jeremiah 3:4,19; 31:9; Malachi 1:6; 2:10.
38   See 2 Samuel 7:14; 1 Chronicles 17:13; 22:10; 28:6; Psalm 68:6; 89:26 for examples.
39   See Exodus 4:22-23; Deuteronomy 1:31; 8:5; 14:1; Psalm 103:13; Jeremiah 3:22; 31:20; Hosea 11:1-4; Malachi 3:17.

Look down from heaven and see. From your holy and glorious habitation. Where are your zeal and your might? The yearning of your heart and your compassion? They are withheld from me. For you are our father, though Abraham does not know us and Israel does not acknowledge us; you, O Lord, are our father; our Redeemer from of old is your name. Why, O Lord, do you make us stray from your ways and harden our heart, so that we do not fear you? Turn back for the sake of your servants, for the sake of the tribes that are your heritage.
Isaiah 65:15-17 (NRSV)

The concept of God as 'father' only actually appears fifteen times in the Old Testament,[40] and it is interesting to note that of those fifteen appearances, only the two quoted from Isaiah are used in direct prayer, the other thirteen are simply adjectives to clarify the meaning of 'God' in some way or another. To be called 'a child of God' in Israel[41] was to be called into relationship with God as part of his chosen people.

The New Testament

Yet in the New Testament, the concept of God as 'Father' erupts into clarity and personal intimacy. The Aramaic term 'Abba' is used three times in the New Testament – and each time it is associated with prayer:

"Abba Father", he cried out, "everything is possible for you. Please take this cup of suffering away from me. Yet I want your will to be done, not mine."
Mark 14:36 (NLT)

"So you have not received a spirit that makes you fearful slaves. Instead, you received God's Spirit when he adopted you as his own children. Now we call him, "Abba, Father."
Romans 8:15 (NLT)

"And because we are his children, God has sent the Spirit of his Son into our hearts, prompting us to call out, "Abba, Father."
Galatians 4:6 (NLT)

This term 'Abba' is one of intimacy and closeness. It takes the concept of God's fatherhood to a whole new level. People often think that the best way to translate it is 'daddy' – but that actually isn't the case. The word carries all the intimacy of the word 'daddy' but it also carries a sense of deep respect and awe, a holy and hushed reverence. The word 'Papa' might be a better way of trying to capture what the word actually means. God is close, intimate, knowable and personal, but he is also holy, challenging and pure. He is not to be taken lightly.

Such intimacy is unheard of in the Old Testament. Yet in the New Testament it is, by far, the clearest and most powerful picture of what God is like. When you bear in mind that the word *'Pater'*, which is only used 15 times in the Old Testament is used over 250 times in the New Testament, you begin to understand just how much clearer the picture of God is for us as Christians.

---

40   The Latin word *'Pater'* is used to capture the idea of 'Father' in the Vulgate version of the Old Testament.
41   See Exodus 4:22; Deuteronomy 14:1; Hosea 11:1.

The fifteenth century Russian artist Andrei Rublev's famous painting of the three angels that visited Abraham on the fields of Mamre has become one of the world's best known images of the Trinity. In it, the three angelic visitors also symbolize the Father, the Son and the Spirit, in intimacy and love and beautifully connected.

Up close and personal

Of course, this picture of God as a personal and knowable Father is most clearly demonstrated by the relationship the Lord Jesus has with his Father.[42] Jesus' use of the language of 'father' and his evident relationship with God the Father ushers in a greater clarity than was ever conceived of in the Old Testament. Indeed the very first recorded words of Jesus and his very last words before his murder both point to God the Father:

He said to them, "Why were you searching for me? Did you not know that I must be in my Father's house?"
Luke 2:49 (NRSV)[43]

Then Jesus, crying with a loud voice, said, "Father, into your hands I commend my spirit." Having said this, he breathed his last.
Luke 23:46 (NRSV)[44]

God the Father talks intimately and personally of his love and pride in his Son at both the baptism of Christ and his transfiguration:

At Jesus' Baptism:

And just as he was coming up out of the water, he saw the heavens torn apart and the Spirit descending like a dove on him. And a voice came from heaven, "You are my Son, the Beloved; with you I am well pleased."
Mark 1:10-11 (NRSV)

At The Transfiguration:

Then a cloud overshadowed them, and from the cloud there came a voice, "This is my Son, the Beloved; listen to him."
Mark 9:7 (NRSV)

It is impossible to reflect on Jesus words and relationship with his Father without reaching the conclusion that we are seeing a deep, personal and beautiful relationship within the heart of God himself. That glimpse into the heart of God then invites us into a powerful and personal intimacy with God for ourselves.

---

42 The figures of Jesus' interaction with God as 'Father' are startling. The language appears 15 times in Mark's Gospel, 9 times in material that is found in both the Gospels of Matthew and Luke, 5 times in material unique to Luke, 18 times in material unique to Matthew and a staggering 117 times in material found in John's Gospel. In John 17 alone Jesus refers to the Father 6 times.
43 When Mary and Joseph discovered Jesus was in the Temple, and not part of the 'caravan trail'.
44 The last words of Christ upon the cross. Immediately after this, the Roman Centurion said, "Certainly this man was innocent".

Personal relationship between us and God the Father

The briefest of glances at the rest of the New Testament leaves us with a powerful invitation to intimacy and personal relationship with God.[45] God invites those who trust in him to enter into a special relationship with their Father:

> BUT TO AS MANY AS DID RECEIVE AND WELCOME HIM, HE GAVE THE AUTHORITY [POWER, PRIVILEGE, RIGHT] TO BECOME THE CHILDREN OF GOD, THAT IS, TO THOSE WHO BELIEVE IN [ADHERE TO, TRUST IN, AND RELY ON] HIS NAME.
>
> John 1:12 (The Amplified Bible)

God, then, has invited us into a deeply personal relationship with himself. In fact, there is a certain challenge in this. Although the New Testament does occasionally show God as the Father of all life and certainly portrays him as the Father of all families,[46] the Lord Jesus only describes God as a Father to those who have responded to his call upon their lives.[47] This doesn't mean that God only loves those who follow him, though. It means that God loves all people and has invited all to experience the intimacy and freedom of a relationship with him. He invites everyone, whether we respond or not is a choice that we must make. If we say 'No' to his invitation, he will let us have our own way.

---

45   See Paul's reflection on this in Romans 1:7; 8:14-17; 15:6 1 Corinthians 1:3; 8:6;2 Corinthians 1:2-3; 11:31; Ephesians 1:3; Galatians 4:1. John picks up the imagery in John 1:12ff, 18; 3:35; 6:57; 8:26-29; 10:15,30; 12:49; 14:7,9,10; 16:15; 1 John 3:1.
46   See Ephesians 3:14; Hebrews 12:9; James 1:17.
47   This is particularly true in the 'Sermon on the Mount' and the 'Sermon on the Plain' but is also evident in other teaching. See Matthew 5:44, 45; 6:8, 32; Matthew 7:11; Mark 11:25; Luke 6:36; 12:32.

What is the impact of God the Father being 'personal'?

When we think about the impact of God as a Father who is 'personal' we quickly discover that this reality is so fundamental that it changes everything.

God The Father:

- 'Source'. God is the Source of our life. Just as any father is a source to his children, so God is the 'Source' of all life.[48]

- 'Sustainer'. God upholds all life.[49]

- 'Adopter'. We are drawn into the family of God and given all the rights and privileges of a birth child when we trust in Christ.[50]

The Personal God:

- God is 'knowable'. He has not left us groping around in the dark trying to work out what he is really like. He has 'revealed' himself to us. God is not simply a force, a power, or an idea, he is a person, with personality traits and characteristics.

- God is 'relational'. He wants to enter into relationship with people. He is not running away from us, he has come to us and longs to be involved in our lives.

TRAGICALLY, FOR MANY OF US THE FATHER-CHILD RELATIONSHIP IS FRAUGHT WITH FEAR, SHAME, DREAD, DISAPPOINTMENT, OR ABSENCE. FOR SOME OF US...THE WORD FATHER HAS BEEN DARKENED BY THE WORST OF EVILS. CAN YOU EVER HOPE TO KNOW GOD AS YOUR FATHER IF YOUR VIEW OF FATHER IS SO BROKEN?

Mike Wilkerson, *Redemption*[51]

The Father who invites us and engages with his world

God does not simply 'exist' in isolation 'somewhere else'. He is intimately and deeply engaged in his world at every level. He sustains the whole creation, but he also sustains us. He sees the challenges we face as individuals, but he also sees the challenges faced by nations, people groups and societies. He reaches out his hand in friendship, love and holiness to me as a person but he also reaches out his hand to families, villages, hamlets, towns and cities. He doesn't simply watch us with an uninterested or an apathetic eye, he watches us with the longing of one who will not impose himself upon us, but instead longs to be invited into our lives. He yearns for relationship with his creation, yet will not force himself upon us. The question is not whether God is interested in our world or our lives, the question is whether we are interested in God. He is so committed to relationship with us that he enters into humanity and endures great suffering and loss for us. Yet still he waits for us to respond to him, still he will not force his hand. He would rather we loved him as his friends than that we cowered before him as his underlings, so he lets us choose.

---

48   The Creation Narratives are the best example of this in the book of Genesis.
49   See Hebrews 1:1-3 or the powerful words of John 13, where Jesus is aware that all things have been 'entrusted' to him by His Father. Of course, Jesus is also described as the Sustainer in Hebrews 1 and in Colossians 1.
50   See Romans 8:14-17.

51   WILKERSON, Mike, Redemption (Wheaton, IL: Crossway, 2011) p. 51.

Does a personal God suffer?

One of the big questions that arises from the soil of believing in a personal God is whether or not God can 'suffer'? If God can suffer then we have a strong point of connection with him in this. Alternatively, if God knows all things and sees all things, then in what way can he suffer? And if he can't suffer, can he genuinely understand us? If he cannot suffer, does that mean that he cannot be entirely personal? The doctrine of whether or not God suffers is known as the 'Passibility' or 'Impassibility' (taken from the Latin word for 'suffer', from which the English word 'Passion', used to describe Easter, derives.)

In his work, *Theology Of The Cross* (1518-19), Martin Luther argued that God must have suffered. He argued that there were two ways of thinking about God. One is a 'theology of glory' and the other is 'a theology of the cross'. Luther deliberately talks about 'God crucified'. This idea was picked up by the German theologian Jurgen Moltmann, in his book, *The Crucified God* written in 1974. Here is an excerpt from that book:

A God who cannot suffer is poorer than any human. For a God who is incapable of suffering is a being who cannot be involved. Suffering and injustice do not affect him. And because he is so completely insensitive, he cannot be affected or shaken by anything. He cannot weep, for he has no tears. But the one who cannot suffer, cannot love either. So he is also a loveless being.[52]

---

52   MOLTMANN, Jurgen, The Crucified God (London: SCM Press, 1974).

What are the implications of a God who cannot suffer? Does this make him impersonal?

How does the idea of a 'suffering God' help you to relate to him?

Do you believe God can suffer? If so, how might he be suffering now?

Letting the personal God impact every area of our lives

It is easy for us to allow our belief about God being 'personal' and 'knowable' to slip into self-centred spirituality, where everything becomes about me. But we are not free to do that. God's revelation of himself to us is so that we might reveal him to others. Think about how the truth of God as 'Father', and as 'Personal' impacts the various aspects of your life and the way you view the world.

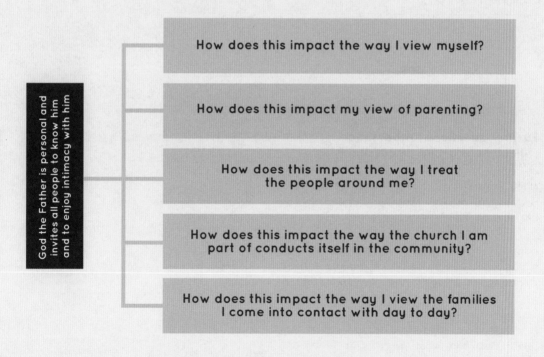

God the Father is personal and invites all people to know him and to enjoy intimacy with him

How does this impact the way I view myself?

How does this impact my view of parenting?

How does this impact the way I treat the people around me?

How does this impact the way the church I am part of conducts itself in the community?

How does this impact the way I view the families I come into contact with day to day?

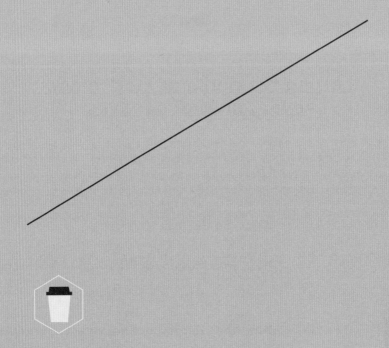

Further questions for personal reflection or group discussion:

Many Christians talk about having a 'personal relationship' with God. What does that mean, and do you think the phrase is over-used?

How can we avoid making the mistake of equating a 'personal' God with a God who agrees with our culture and fits in with our views and our lives?

Discuss or think about your own 'personal' relationship with God. How do you sustain that relationship and what do you do when the relationship breaks down?

If God is 'personal' does that make him 'private'? Can you have a personal faith in God that does not have public consequences? In what ways do you think you might be hiding your relationship with God from those around you, and what can you do about it?

Lessons from Mackesy and Rembrandt

The amazing invitation to encounter God as a loving and caring Father has captured the hearts of many artists through the years. Perhaps the most famous painting of this is Rembrandt's, which hangs in the Hermitage Gallery. Another is the bronze statue by the British artist Charlie Mackesy. As you look at these images, reflect on the following words from Henri Nouwen's reflection on the painting by Rembrandt:

For most of my life I have struggled to find God, to know God, to love God. I have tried hard to follow the guidelines of the spiritual life—pray always, work for others, read the Scriptures—and to avoid the many temptations to dissipate myself. I have failed many times but always tried again, even when I was close to despair.

Now I wonder whether I have sufficiently realized that during all this time God has been trying to find me, to know me, and to love me. The question is not "How am I to find God?" but "How am I to let myself be found by him?" The question is not "How am I to know God?" but "How am I to let myself be known by God?" And, finally, the question is not "How am I to love God?" but "How am I to let myself be loved by God?" God is looking into the distance for me, trying to find me, and longing to bring me home.
Henri Nouwen, *The Return of the Prodigal Son, A Story of Homecoming*[53]

---

53   NOUWEN, Henri, The Return Of The Prodigal Son: A Story Of Homecoming (New York: Doubleday, 1992).

GOD, THE FATHER ALMIGHTY IS POWERFUL

We do not only believe that God the Father is personal, we also believe that he is Almighty God. The second part of the affirmation of the Apostles' Creed that was explored in the Bible Study this morning states:

I BELIEVE IN GOD, THE FATHER ALMIGHTY, CREATOR OF HEAVEN AND EARTH.

To believe in a personal God who is powerless is of little use to anyone. God is not limited by our conception of him. Belief in an 'Almighty' or omnipotent God is an essential element of traditional Christian thought. But what does it mean to believe in God, the Father Almighty, Creator of heaven and earth and what are the implications of believing it?

Omnipotence

A basic definition of omnipotence would be something like this: If God is omnipotent, then he can do anything. Of course, God cannot make a stone too big for himself to carry. He cannot make a square circle or a round square – such illogical statements are simply glorified self-contradictions. To talk of Almighty God or God as omnipotent is to talk of a God who can do *anything which does not involve illogical contradiction.*

The Bible and God's almighty power

There are repeated references in the Bible to God being able to do the impossible.[54] From his work in Creation (and note that we believe in *God, the Father Almighty, Creator of heaven and earth,*[55]) to his work in resurrection,[56] and his ultimate work of re-creating the whole earth,[57] God is portrayed as a Gardener who is in the business of making, restoring and ultimately completely recreating the world. Two of the clearest examples of his declaration of his own power are found in Psalm 18 and in Job 38-42 respectively. In the latter, God declares his greatness and his power through a series of great rhetorical questions:

Where were you when I laid the foundation of the earth?

Who shut in the sea with doors?

Have you commanded the morning since your days began?

Have you entered into the springs of the sea or walked in the recesses of the deep?
Job 38:4,8,12,16 (NRSV)

---

54   For example, see Matthew 19:26; Mark 14:36; Luke 1:37; Jeremiah 10:12; 32:27; Isaiah 40:28; 44:24; Job 37:23; 42:2; Psalm 147:5; Daniel 4:35 Romans 1:20; 8:28-29; Mark 10:27; 1 Corinthians 1:25 Hebrews 1:3; Revelation 19:6; Ephesians 1:19-22 etc.
55   See Genesis 1-3.
56   See John 20:1-3.
57   See Revelation 21.

When confronted with the power of Rome in the reign of Pontius Pilate, Jesus candidly told Pilate:

You would have no power over me at all unless it were given to you from above.
John 19:11 (NLT)

It is clear from Scripture that God is to be seen as *Almighty*. He is the *Creator* of heaven and earth. Nothing, therefore, is beyond his power or his ability.

Implications of God as Creator of the heavens and the earth

There are some immediate implications that arise out of the concept of God as Creator for us as Christians.

1. If God is Creator, then the universe and everything in it has an origin. We are not an accident, we are part of a divine plan.

2. If we are part of a *planned* creation, then we are wanted.

3. If God is the Creator of the *heavens* and the earth, then there is another dimension to life that we cannot see fully at the moment.

4. If God is the Creator of the heavens and the earth then the earth itself matters and how we treat it is an issue that we must take seriously.

5. If God is the Creator of the heavens and the *earth,* then nothing is beyond his power or control. If that is so, why do bad things happen?

The Irish writer C.S. Lewis explored the question of God's omnipotence and power in his masterpiece, *The Problem Of Pain:*

If God were good, he would wish to make his creatures perfectly happy, and if God were Almighty he would be able to do what he wished. But the creatures are not happy. Therefore God lacks either the goodness, or power, or both. This is the problem of pain in its simplest form.[58]

The question is, however, what do we mean when we describe God as 'omnipotent' or 'Almighty'? Actually, it doesn't mean that God can do anything because once God decides on certain actions, or to behave in a certain way, he voluntarily limits himself. Here is Lewis again:

If you choose to say, "God can give a creature free will and at the same time withhold free will from it", you have not succeeded in saying anything about God: meaningless combinations of words do not suddenly acquire a meaning because we prefix to them two other words: "God can". It remains true that all things are possible with God: The intrinsic impossibilities are not things but non-entities.[59]

---

58   LEWIS, C.S., The Problem Of Pain (London: The Centenary Press, 1942).
59   Ibid.

God may be 'Almighty' then, but he will not do anything that is logically impossible and nor will he do anything that is contrary to or inconsistent with, his nature. The implications of this are profound:

- Having given humanity free-will, God will not force us to choose him.

- Having entrusted the creation to humanity to govern and steward, God will not take it back from us and do the job for us.

- The past cannot be undone, even by God, despite the fact that it can be redeemed.

Listen to the words of Anselm of Canterbury as he wrestles with this question:

How can you be omnipotent, if you cannot do all things? But how can you do all things, if you cannot be corrupted, or tell lies, or make the true into false?...Or is the ability to do these things not power but powerlessness?
Anselm of Canterbury, *Proslogion*[60]

Another way of looking at this is to think of it in terms of what happens when there is an absence of power rather than a presence of power. Why can God not lie? Is it because he is powerless or powerful? Of course, it is because he is powerful. Telling lies is the result of *powerlessness* and an *inability* to remain truthful. Another example is sinning. To 'sin' is to fall short, to fail, to stumble, to miss the mark. All of these images and metaphors try to capture the idea of sin as a 'weakness'. Because God does not have such weakness, he cannot sin. His *power* means he cannot sin.

Almighty power... self-limiting God

The phrase 'Almighty God' then, means that God, who is all-powerful, has actually limited himself because of the freedoms he has given humanity and the way in which he has created the world.

In short, that means that although God can do anything, he doesn't do everything we want or we think is right because he has released some of his power to us as his creation. This idea of *self-limitation* in Almighty God can be seen clearly in Paul's description of Jesus 'emptying himself'[61] found in Philippians 2:6-7:

Though he was in the form of God, [he] did not regard equality with God as something to be exploited, but emptied himself, taking the form of a slave, being born in human likeness. And being found in human form, he humbled himself and became obedient to the point of death - even death on a cross.
Philippians 2:6-7 (NRSV)

Dietrich Bonhoeffer, the Germany martyr of the Second World War, puts it this way:

God lets himself be pushed out of the world on the cross. He is weak and powerless in the world, and that is precisely the way, the only way, in which he is with us and helps us...The Bible directs us to God's powerlessness and suffering; only the suffering God can help.
Dietrich Bonhoeffer, *Letters And Papers From Prison*[62]

---

60   S. ANSELM OF CANTERBURY, Proslogion: Including Gaunilo's Objections And Anselm's Replies Translated And Introduced By Matthew D. Waltz, (South Bend, IN., 2013).

61   The Greek term is kenosis.
62   BONHOEFFER, Dietrich, Letters And Papers From Prison (New York: SCM Press, 1971).

The implications of an Almighty but self-limiting Creator

Of course, the implications of a God who is all powerful, yet at the same time gives up some of his power, are immense for us:

- He entrusts us with the responsibility of caring for the Creation.

- He asks us to model his fatherhood into our families and our society faithfully.

- Whilst he is in control of all things, he has permitted pain in the world because the cost of removing it would be the removal of our freedom and our freedom is too precious to be relinquished.

- He ultimately invites us into relationship with himself but does not force us into that relationship.

- The consequence of entering a relationship with him is that we follow him, obey him and love him in our lives, our communities, our nations and ultimately in the created world.

- The consequence of not entering into a relationship with him is that we do what we want and face the consequences of the actions that we choose in our lives, our communities, our nations and ultimately in the created world.

Do we need to change to be acceptable to God?

One of the deepest questions we can face as we think about God is whether we need to change before he will accept us or whether we can just stay as we are?

Such a question is posed in terms that are not helpful, because neither option explains the way in which God engages with us. The personal and the powerful God comes to us and reveals himself to us so that we might make a response to him. There is absolutely no doubt that he accepts us just as we are. He loves us just as we are. He embraces us just as we are. Even a cursory look at the lives of people such as Nicodemus,[63] Mary Magdalene,[64] Zacchaeus[65] or the woman at the well[66] shows us that God accepts us as we are. Yet a closer examination of the stories of these people shows us something very important. Jesus undoubtedly accepted them where they were, but he also encouraged them, or commanded them, to change. Nicodemus was challenged to cast off his religious views and enter into relationship with God, Mary was delivered of her demonic spirits and became a devoted follower of Christ, Zacchaeus abandoned his selfish and greedy lifestyle and restored the goods and money he had taken unfairly, and the woman at the well was challenged about the nature of her private lifestyle as Jesus talked with her.

The reality is that God accepts us where we are, but he also gives us the power to change. In God's purposes and plans, no one is exempt from the invitation to come and no is exempt from the possibility of change. Such is the power of the Father and such is his longing for us. He loves us enough to accept us where we are. He is powerful enough to change the deepest parts of our lives so that we might be truly free.

---

63   You can read more about the story of Jesus' encounter with Nicodemus in John 3.
64   You can read more about Mary Magdalene in Luke 8, John 19 &20, Mark 15 & 16.
65   You can read more about Zacchaeus in Luke 19.
66   You can read more about the woman at the well in John 4.

<u>Letting the powerful God impact</u>
<u>every area of our lives</u>

It is easy for us to allow our belief about God being 'powerful' and 'all-present' to slip into detached spirituality, where everything becomes about someone else. But we are not free to do that. God's revelation of himself to us is so that we might reveal him to others. Think about how the truth of God as 'father', and as 'powerful' impacts the various aspects of your life and the way you view the world.

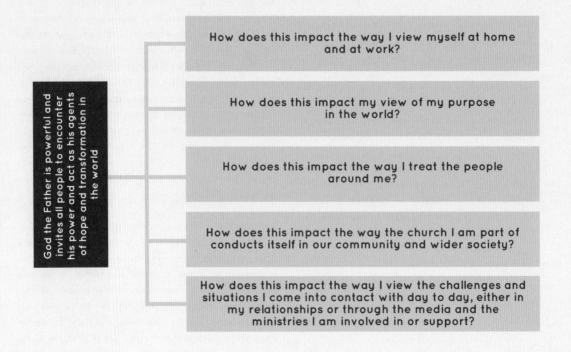

God the Father is powerful and invites all people to encounter his power and act as his agents of hope and transformation in the world

How does this impact the way I view myself at home and at work?

How does this impact my view of my purpose in the world?

How does this impact the way I treat the people around me?

How does this impact the way the church I am part of conducts itself in our community and wider society?

How does this impact the way I view the challenges and situations I come into contact with day to day, either in my relationships or through the media and the ministries I am involved in or support?

Each evening, during our celebrations, we will be inviting you to go beyond 'studying' the issue we have been facing each day and to enter into an encounter with God. To do that, we will be using Jesus' powerful words of hope, comfort and challenge to his disciples contained in his parting address to them. This is known as The Farewell Discourse and is found in the Gospel of John in chapters 14-17. We will also be using Psalm 46 to help us encounter God.

Why not take a few moments either before or after the evening celebration to reflect on the words of both of these passages and to ask God to either prepare you for what he wants to do in your life and heart or to confirm what he has done as you prepare to sleep.

THE FATHER WE LONG FOR

This is the enemy's one central purpose – to separate us from the Father. He uses neglect to whisper, "You see, no one cares. You're not worth caring about." He uses a sudden loss of innocence to whisper, "This is a dangerous world, and you are alone. You've been abandoned"... And in this way he makes it nearly impossible for us to know what Jesus knew, makes it so very, very hard to come to the Father's heart towards us.
John Eldredge, *Fathered By God*[67]

This evening, as we focus on 'the Father we long for' there are a couple of ways in which we could miss what God wants to do.

The first is to think that the issue of God as our Father is only about us. To do that would mean we turn God into our personal Source, Sustainer and Adopter at the expense of the world around us. If we aren't careful, this can actually lead to us being so caught up with ourselves that we miss the challenges and the opportunities before us.

The second is to think that our own personal relationship with God as our Father doesn't matter at all and that we can just focus on loving others and helping them. That's also not true, because it leaves a great big gaping hole in our hearts and our lives that forces us to minister and serve out of a need to fill that space. That's never healthy. We don't minister to others what we have not received ourselves. We don't need to earn God's acceptance.

Instead, ask yourself where the key areas of your own understanding of the father-heart of God for you and for the world around you need to be changed and strengthened. Perhaps these questions might help:

- What aspects of God's father-heart do you desperately need to experience again (or even for the first time)?

- Where can the father-heart of God be most powerfully demonstrated through you to those around you?

- How can your own personal journey in this area be used as a great blessing to others so that they might experience the grace and mercy of God?

67   ELDREDGE, John, Fathered By God, (Nashville, TN: Thomas Nelson, 2009) pp. 57-58.

Father,
That one word changes everything.
To know that you are my Father and not my oppressor helps me reach out to you.
To know that you are tender and not harsh helps me not to be afraid of you.
To know that you accept me enough to love me right where I am helps me to lift up my head
before you.

To know that you love me enough to change me helps me not to feel trapped.
To know that you are powerful helps me to have hope.
To know that you are personal helps me to understand you.
To know that you are interested in my life helps me know that I matter.
To know that you are interested in our world helps me make a difference.

So father me, Lord.
Father the real me.
The broken me.
The messed-up me.
The confused me.
The angry me.
Don't father the pretend me.
Don't bolster up the me I want everyone else to see.
Come in your grace and power and undo the perfect version of me I try to present to the world.

Come and meet me as me.
Change me that I might be like you.
Love like you.
Speak like you.
Act like you.
Live like you.

Take me, Father.
Take all of me.
And let me find myself
My real self
My beautiful, vulnerable, honest and truthful self,
In you.

Amen

The Unbeatable Son

The Big Start

"The Son who sets us free!"

The Unbeatable Son

"Together with Christ, we are heirs..."

Romans 8:17 (NLT)

Celebrations

Without him, we can do nothing

Bible Study

"I believe in Jesus Christ, his only Son, our Lord..."

Spaces and Seminars

The God who loves us saves us. He is both tangible and tender

— THE SON WHO SETS US FREE —

This morning in the Big Start we'll be exploring the fact that the Lord Jesus is able to break every single chain that ties us down. There is nothing too hard for him. Sometimes we can allow ourselves to get trapped and we can think that there is no way out, but that is not true. Nothing is impossible for Jesus.

This is most powerfully shown in the fact that Jesus raised people from the dead, and that he himself was resurrected. We will be exploring the powerful reality of resurrection this morning as we begin our day today.

In Minehead 1 & 3 and in Skegness we will be exploring this great idea of 'The Son who sets us Free' by looking at the story of Jesus' resurrection itself, told in John 20:1-23. In Minehead 2, we will be taking an extra day to also explore the story of the raising of Lazarus from the dead, told in John 11:17-44.

Why not take a few moments at the beginning of the day to read these passages and to ask God to powerfully encounter you as an individual, as a church, or as a family. How can you celebrate that you have been set free today?

The resurrection of Jesus

Early on Sunday morning, while it was still dark, Mary Magdalene came to the tomb and found that the stone had been rolled away from the entrance. She ran and found Simon Peter and the other disciple, the one whom Jesus loved. She said, "They have taken the Lord's body out of the tomb, and we don't know where they have put him!"

Peter and the other disciple started out for the tomb. They were both running, but the other disciple outran Peter and reached the tomb first. He stooped and looked in and saw the linen wrappings lying there, but he didn't go in. Then Simon Peter arrived and went inside. He also noticed the linen wrappings lying there, while the cloth that had covered Jesus' head was folded up and lying apart from the other wrappings. Then the disciple who had reached the tomb first also went in, and he saw and believed - for until then they still hadn't understood the Scriptures that said Jesus must rise from the dead. Then they went home.

Mary was standing outside the tomb crying, and as she wept, she stooped and looked in. She saw two white-robed angels, one sitting at the head and the other at the foot of the place where the body of Jesus had been lying. "Dear woman, why are you crying?" the angels asked her.

"Because they have taken away my Lord," she replied, "and I don't know where they have put him."

She turned to leave and saw someone standing there. It was Jesus, but she didn't recognize him. "Dear woman, why are you crying?" Jesus asked her. "Who are you looking for?"

She thought he was the gardener. "Sir," she said, "if you have taken him away, tell me where you have put him, and I will go and get him."

"Mary!" Jesus said.

She turned to him and cried out, "Rabboni!" (which is Hebrew for "Teacher").

"Don't cling to me," Jesus said, "for I haven't yet ascended to the Father. But go, find my brothers and tell them, 'I am ascending to my Father and your Father, to my God and your God.'"

Mary Magdalene found the disciples and told them, "I have seen the Lord!" Then she gave them his message.

That Sunday evening the disciples were meeting behind locked doors because they were afraid of the Jewish leaders. Suddenly, Jesus was standing there among them! "Peace be with you," he said. As he spoke, he showed them the wounds in his hands and his side. They were filled with joy when they saw the Lord! Again he said, "Peace be with you. As the Father has sent me, so I am sending you." Then he breathed on them and said, "Receive the Holy Spirit. If you forgive anyone's sins, they are forgiven. If you do not forgive them, they are not forgiven."
John 20:1-23 (NLT)

The resurrection of Lazarus

When Jesus arrived at Bethany, he was told that Lazarus had already been in his grave for four days. Bethany was only a few miles down the road from Jerusalem, and many of the people had come to console Martha and Mary in their loss. When Martha got word that Jesus was coming, she went to meet him. But Mary stayed in the house. Martha said to Jesus, "Lord, if only you had been here, my brother would not have died. But even now I know that God will give you whatever you ask."

Jesus told her, "Your brother will rise again."

"Yes," Martha said, "he will rise when everyone else rises, at the last day."

Jesus told her, "I am the resurrection and the life. Anyone who believes in me will live, even after dying. Everyone who lives in me and believes in me will never ever die. Do you believe this, Martha?"

"Yes, Lord," she told him. "I have always believed you are the Messiah, the Son of God, the one who has come into the world from God." Then she returned to Mary. She called Mary aside from the mourners and told her, "The Teacher is here and wants to see you." So Mary immediately went to him.

Jesus had stayed outside the village, at the place where Martha met him. When the people who were at the house consoling Mary saw her leave so hastily, they assumed she was going to Lazarus's grave to weep. So they followed her there. When Mary arrived and saw Jesus, she fell at his feet and said, "Lord, if only you had been here, my brother would not have died."

When Jesus saw her weeping and saw the other people wailing with her, a deep anger welled up within him, and he was deeply troubled. "Where have you put him?" he asked them.

They told him, "Lord, come and see." Then Jesus wept. The people who were standing nearby said, "See how much he loved him!" But some said, "This man healed a blind man. Couldn't he have kept Lazarus from dying?"

Jesus was still angry as he arrived at the tomb, a cave with a stone rolled across its entrance. "Roll the stone aside," Jesus told them.

But Martha, the dead man's sister, protested, "Lord, he has been dead for four days. The smell will be terrible."

Jesus responded, "Didn't I tell you that you would see God's glory if you believe?" So they rolled the stone aside. Then Jesus looked up to heaven and said, "Father, thank you for hearing me. You always hear me, but I said it out loud for the sake of all these people standing here, so that they will believe you sent me." Then Jesus shouted, "Lazarus, come out!" And the dead man came out, his hands and feet bound in grave clothes, his face wrapped in a headcloth. Jesus told them, "Unwrap him and let him go!"

John 11:17-44 (NLT)

— WE BELIEVE IN JESUS CHRIST, — HIS ONLY SON, OUR LORD

The Bible study today will explore the second statement of the Apostles' Creed[68]:

I BELIEVE IN JESUS CHRIST,
HIS ONLY SON, OUR LORD,
WHO WAS CONCEIVED BY THE HOLY SPIRIT,
BORN OF THE VIRGIN MARY,
SUFFERED UNDER PONTIUS PILATE,
WAS CRUCIFIED, DIED, AND WAS BURIED;
HE DESCENDED TO THE DEAD.
ON THE THIRD DAY HE ROSE AGAIN;
HE ASCENDED INTO HEAVEN,
HE IS SEATED AT THE RIGHT HAND
OF THE FATHER,
AND HE WILL COME TO JUDGE
THE LIVING AND THE DEAD.

In Minehead 1 & 3 and Skegness, we will be taking this whole part of the Apostles' Creed as the basis of our Bible Study on Morning 3, but in Minehead 2, we will be splitting the study of the truths behind this statement into two sections. On Day 3, we will explore the following part:

I believe in Jesus Christ, his only Son, our Lord,
who was conceived by the Holy Spirit,
born of the Virgin Mary,
suffered under Pontius Pilate,
was crucified, died, and was buried;
he descended to the dead.

And on Day 4, we will explore the following part:

On the third day he rose again;
he ascended into heaven,
he is seated at the right hand of the Father,
and he will come to judge the living and the dead.

This part of the Apostles' Creed makes such powerful statements about what we believe about God and his relationship with us that it would be impossible to over-estimate their importance. At its heart, Christianity has an absolute commitment to the unique revelation of God through his Son, the Lord Jesus Christ. He is not simply one of a number of options for approaching God, he is God's 'only Son'. The Christian faith sets him apart and above all and any other revelation of God to us.

He is not simply a good example, a moral man, an interesting metaphor or an ethical consultant – he is God in human flesh. He is God himself, come down to earth to live and walk amongst us.

---

68   The life, ministry and Lordship of Jesus Christ can be explored in passages such as Genesis 3:15; Isaiah 53, 61; Matthew 1; Luke 1,4; 1 Corinthians 15:3-11; John 1; Romans 8; Colossians 2.

Unpacking this part of orthodox Christian teaching lies at the heart of what is truly held to be Christian doctrine.

- Jesus is the unique revelation of God to us.
- Jesus is our Lord.
- Jesus was conceived of the Holy Spirit and born of a virgin.
- Jesus actually lived and died – he was a real person in time and history and lived within a specific context. He knows the limitations of humanity as well as its joys.
- Jesus tasted actual death and was buried physically as well as entering death spiritually.
- Jesus overcame death and rose again. He physically and spiritually conquered the greatest enemy and deepest fear of all people – sin and death themselves.
- Jesus' ministry continues now as he is with his Father in Heaven and is interceding and praying for us.
- Jesus will return one day as the righteous judge of all the earth and every single human being that has ever lived will stand before him.

Although these truths are some of the most important and distinctive in Christian faith, they are also some of the most debated and discussed and controversial. How can we claim that Jesus is a unique revelation of God in the midst of so many other religious groups and movements? What possible sense does the virgin birth make today and why does it matter? Why would a loving God cause his Son to suffer at the hands of the Roman Empire and die such a cruel death? Why didn't God intervene and save his Son? Is it reasonable or sensible to believe in resurrection?

Heaven is surely just a state of mind, it couldn't possibly be a place as well as a dimension, could it? Isn't it unreasonable and offensive to talk of God 'judging' people – let alone the incredible suggestion that all people that have ever been will face such a judgement?

There are many who would hope that a new Apostles' Creed might be introduced. One that talks about a Jesus who fits in with our culture and our world. Yet the Apostles' Creed sets out the deep truths of our affirmations of the ministry and life of Jesus – and it also seems to miss some things!

Nothing of the life of Jesus? Nothing of Israel? Nothing of the Kingdom of God? Nothing of his words and movements and living amongst ordinary people? Nothing of his miraculous ministry, his challenging of the Roman Empire and his deliberate and wilful confrontation of the religious controllers and leaders of Israel? Nothing about his ministry to the poor and the broken? Why these absences?

Which comes first, the Gospels or the Creed?

This is where our Bible study becomes so vital. We are not seeking to read the Gospels by way of the Creed. If we do that we will miss the point of the Gospels themselves, their amazing and life changing declaration that Jesus is the King of a new Kingdom and he calls us to be his subjects and demonstrate the power and the life of this new realm right here and right now! If we seek to read the Creed by way of the Gospel story, then we will understand it as we should.

Is it possible that this section of the Creed underpins so much of our thinking, yet also summarises rather than articulates everything? What if the part of the Creed which states that the Lord Jesus was 'born of the Virgin Mary and suffered under Pontius Pilate' actually includes everything in between in his earthly ministry and therefore incorporates the hopes and longings of Israel in a Messiah and the purpose and power of the Kingdom?

Our Bible study will help us to see that the physical, flesh and blood ministry of Jesus, his extraordinary claims, his virgin birth, his Kingdom and sinless life, his atoning death, his physical death and resurrection, his ascended ministry and his promised return are all part of the non-negotiable convictions of traditional Christian faith.

Without upholding the centrality of Jesus, we lose the right to call ourselves his followers and we forfeit the privilege of using the word 'Christian'.

THE GOD WHO LOVES US SAVES US

Eugene Peterson on the centrality of Jesus:

And so Jesus is my text for cultivating a language that honours the holiness inherent in words: the God-rootedness, the Christ-embodiedness, the Spirit-aliveness...as we listen in on Jesus as he talks and then participate with Jesus as he prays, I hope that together we...will develop a discerning aversion to all forms of depersonalizing Godtalk and acquire a taste for and skills in the always personal language that God uses, even in our conversations and small talk, maybe especially in our small talk, to make and save and bless us one and all.[69]

P.T. Forsyth on the centrality of Jesus:

There is nothing we are told more often by those who would discard an evangelical faith than this – that we must now do what scholarship has only just enabled us to do, and return to the religion of Jesus. We are bidden to go back to practice Jesus' own personal religion, as distinct from the Gospel of Christ, from a Gospel which calls him its faith's object, and not its subject, founder or classic only. We must learn to believe not in Christ but with Christ...

Let us observe what is the effect of the most recent views about the origin of Christianity upon this point, upon the plea that the first form of Christianity was the so-called religion of Jesus. I refer to the new religious-historical school of Germany...There is one great service which the religious-historical school has rendered. It has destroyed the fiction of the nineteenth century *that there was ever a time in the earliest history of the Church when it cultivated the religion of Jesus as distinct from the Gospel of Christ. The school, of course, may believe itself able to insulate that religion of Jesus and cultivate it, to disengage it from the gospels by a critical process, and preach it to a world pining for a simple creed rescued from the Apostles. That is another matter which I do not here discuss. But it is a great thing to have it settled, as far as the face value of our record goes, and apart from elaborate critical constructions of them, such imitation of the faith of Jesus never existed in the very first Church; that, as far back as we can go, we find only the belief and worship of a risen, redeeming and glorified Christ, whom they could wholly trust but only very poorly imitate; and in his relation to God could not imitate at all.[70]*

69 PETERSON, Eugene, The Word Made Flesh: The Language Of Jesus In His Stories And Prayers (London: Hodder & Stoughton, 2008) p. 5.

70 FORSYTH, Peter Taylor, The Person And Place Of Jesus Christ (London: Independent Press, 1909) pp. 35, 41, 44.

What does it mean to believe in Jesus Christ?

Does just making the statement "I am a Christian" mean that I am a follower of Jesus Christ? Is it okay simply to say that you 'believe in Jesus' and then not evidence that belief in any of your behaviours, attitudes or actions? What does it mean to say, "I believe in Jesus Christ, his only Son, our Lord..."?

When the Philippian jailer asked Paul and Silas, "Sirs, what must I do to be saved?" Paul and Silas replied, "Believe on the Lord Jesus, and you will be saved."[71] To believe means to have faith, to construct your life around the convictions that you hold. There are different kinds of 'faith' and 'believing':

1. Believing that something is historically true.
2. Believing that something is intellectually true.
3. Believing in a set of doctrines or statements.
4. Believing as a spiritual gift.[72]
5. Believing as a core and permanent value, alongside loving and being hopeful.[73]
6. Believing as a way of life that shapes your attitudes, your actions and your character.

It seems quite clear that it is possible to believe in God yet not trust him.[74] It also seems quite clear that you can believe all of God's promises but not live in them and allow them to change your attitude and actions.[75] Whilst belief in the existence of God is vital for Christian faith, as is the conviction that God will meet with us if we seek him, there is a third element of 'believing' that is vital for the Christian life and that is a personal and living response to the truths of Christianity.[76]

When we say, *"I believe in Jesus Christ, his only Son, our Lord..."* then, we are acknowledging that Christ lived and died, that his statements about himself and the world are true and that we are seeking to live out a commitment and submission to those convictions – even if we sometimes fail and falter.

Faith always looks like something

In our 'Spaces' today, we want to explore what faith in the Lord Jesus Christ looks like. Our convictions about Christ should shape our lives and witness for Christ. Whether that be in our homes, in our workplaces, in our schools and universities or in our church families, our belief in the person and work of the Lord Jesus Christ always looks like something. We want to explore three aspects of who Jesus is in our spaces today:

- **God the Son is tangible:** That means that when Jesus was born, the Son of God took on skin and bone, flesh and blood, and he shows us what God is really like in ways that we can both understand and relate to.

- **God the Son is tender:** Although strong and powerful and fully divine, Christ is also tender and gentle. He comes as a servant, not as a master, and he comes to us in grace and truth.

- **God the Son is able to transform us:** Jesus doesn't only understand our situations or the challenges of our planet, he has come to utterly transform our lives and the world in which we live, not just to be sympathetic towards us and our world.

---

71   See Acts 16:26-40 for the full account, and vv. 30ff in particular.
72   See 1 Corinthians 12:9.
73   See 1 Corinthians 13.
74   According to the Epistle of James (see James 2:19) even demons 'believe in God' in this way.
75   For example, Hebrews 11:6 would indicate that for faith to be active and effective in our lives, it must be used.
76   These three elements of belief – (1) Belief in the existence of God; (2) Belief that God invites you to respond to him; (3) Making a believing response of submission and obedience to the truths and reality of God – are all seen in the story recorded in John 4:46-53 of a nobleman who comes to Jesus seeking healing and help for the nobleman's son.

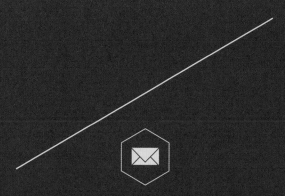

Lord,

I often find myself 'believing' in you historically and treating you like a relic of the past. I listen to what you said and read of who you were and what you did, but I somehow do not let that reality shape the way I make decisions today. I find myself making choices then asking you what you think, instead of asking you to shape my choices in the first place.

I don't want my faith to be an intellectual exercise or an interesting lesson in history. I want my belief in you to shape the way I behave at work. I need you to bring me back to the basic reality of what following Jesus looks like in the office, on the street, in my neighbourhood and in my family life.

Help me to surrender to your ways.

I raise the flag of surrender and lay my own desires and plans down at your feet again.

Help me become more like Jesus rather than just knowing more about him.

Amen.

Who is Jesus Christ?

In 2013, the theme of Spring Harvest was 'The Source: Encountering Jesus Today'. In our Bible Studies, we explored the First Epistle of John. Our aim was to talk about who Jesus was and how we connect to him today and live out our faith in him. Listening to the recordings of the Bible Studies from 2013 will help you to think more about this subject.

This issue is also explored in this year's Theme Book *Unbelievable: Confident Faith In A Sceptical World*.

Trying to understand the Second Person of the Trinity

Christians often get confused about Jesus. Did he always exist? If he did, then where was he before he was Jesus of Nazareth? And where is he now? We talk about Jesus coming to earth – what do we mean by that?

There is a basic answer to the question, but it can get a bit complicated because it involves the concept of the Trinity. Traditional Christian teaching believes that God exists as One God, but in three 'persons' – the Father, the Son and the Holy Spirit. This three-fold existence has always been and will always be. There has never been a point nor will there ever be one when there was no Father; there has never been a point nor will there ever be one when there was no Son; there has never been a point nor will there ever be one when there was no Spirit. You can see glimpses of this eternal relationship of mutual and ongoing love and voluntary dependence all through the Bible. For example:

- In Creation, the Father creates, the Son is the Word spoken and the Spirit is the Breath that carries the Word.[77]

- In Jesus' baptism[78] and at his transfiguration.[79]

So what about Jesus? Has he always existed? Well, the answer is that the Second Person of the Trinity has always existed as the Son, or the Word, or the *logos*.[80] This Second Person of the Trinity 'takes on' flesh in the person of Jesus of Nazareth. God the Living Word, God the Logos, God the 'Son' becomes a human in the person who is named Jesus of Nazareth. From the moment of his 'conception' in the womb of the Virgin Mary, God the Son is Jesus of Nazareth and having become 'flesh and blood' and having 'moved into the neighbourhood'[81] the Second Person of the Trinity continues to be seen in the now-resurrected and perfectly glorified body of the Lord Jesus Christ, who is just as much alive now as he has ever been and continues to be 'enrobed' in human flesh (albeit is now resurrected and transformed human flesh). This means that the resurrected Jesus is our assurance of our own physical and whole resurrection too.

If we want to know what God is really like, we see him in the life, example, ministry and face of Jesus Christ:

We declare to you what was from the beginning, what we have heard, what we have seen with our eyes, what we have looked at and touched with our hands, concerning the word of life – this life was revealed, and we have seen it and testify to it, and declare to you the eternal life that was with the Father and was revealed to us – we declare to you what we have seen and heard so that you may have fellowship with us; and truly our fellowship is with the Father and with His Son Jesus Christ.
1 John 1:1-3 (NRSV)

---

77 See Genesis 1.
78 See Mark 1:9-11.
79 See Mark 9:2-8.
80 *Logos* is a Greek term that means 'reason for all things' or 'the glue that holds all things together' or 'the ultimate word behind all thought and purpose' and is used in John 1, where John tells the story of creation but does so to show that the Second Person of the Trinity was present and active in creation and that this Person is seen in Jesus of Nazareth.

81 Particularly see John 1:14 in The Message.

God the Son is tangible

REGARDLESS OF WHAT ANYONE MAY PERSONALLY THINK OR BELIEVE ABOUT HIM, JESUS OF NAZARETH HAS BEEN THE DOMINANT FIGURE IN THE HISTORY OF WESTERN CULTURE FOR ALMOST TWENTY CENTURIES.

Jaroslav Pelican, *Jesus Through The Centuries*[82]

Jesus Christ is the centre of history. A very large part of the world continues to divide its understanding of time using the abbreviations 'B.C.' and 'A.D.' meaning 'before Christ' and *'anno domini* [the year of the Lord]' respectively. Around one third of the world's population are followers of Jesus.

Jesus is also the focus of the Bible. The Christian Scriptures are not a vague and haphazard collection of books, letters, poems and songs. They have the central focus of Jesus himself. Indeed, as a Jew, Jesus highlighted that the Hebrew Scriptures pointed to him.[83] Christians through the centuries have often acknowledged that if we are ignorant of the Bible, then we will be ignorant of Jesus.[84] Erasmus, the 16th century thinker, wrote;

The Bible will give Christ to you in an intimacy so close that he would be less visible to you if he stood before your eyes.[85]

In his comments on Romans 1:5, Martin Luther said:

Here the door is thrown open wide for the understanding of Holy Scripture, that is, that everything must be understood in relation to Christ.[86]

Thirdly, Jesus is the heart of true Christian mission. Our task is always, and with humility and grace, to continue saying to the people around us, 'Consider Jesus.' He is our message.[87]

For these reasons, and many more, we must come to terms with the God that comes to meet us in the person and ministry of the Lord Jesus himself. We cannot make up a Jesus to suit our culture or water down who Jesus is to make him more acceptable to those around us. Nor can we make him a tyrannical and fearful despot who lashes out at sinners and speaks with venom and anger at the world. Neither of these pictures of Jesus are evident in the Bible. Instead, we meet a Jesus who is knowable, discernable and approachable; a Jesus whom we can relate to. If we look at the bookshelves of Christian theology, we will discover there are many pictures of Jesus that justify the culture or context of the day in which they were written. Yet we, the Bride of Christ, are promised to the Christ who actually lived and breathed and walked amongst us, the One who reaches out to us from Heaven and reveals what he is like through his earthly ministry as recorded, accurately and clearly, in the New Testament.

82   PELIKAN, Jarolsav, Jesus Through The Centuries: His Place In The History Of Culture, (London: Yale University Press, 1985), p. 1.
83   See John 5:39.
84   Saint Jerome said, "Ignorance of the Scriptures is ignorance of Christ". See Jerome's prologue to his Commentary on Isaiah which is quoted in paragraph 25 of Vatican II's 'Dogmatic Constitution On Divine Relationship' in CHAPMAN, Geoffrey: The Documents of Vatican II (Kansas: Angelus Press, 1966).
85   Written in the introduction to Erasmus' Greek New Testament of 1516.
86   See Volume 25 ('Lectures on Romans') in Luther's Works (1515: ET, Concordia, 1972).
87   See NEILL, Bishop Stephen C., Christian Faith And Other Faiths (Oxford: Oxford University Press, 1961) p. 69.

In what ways is Jesus tangible?

We have no need to guess about what Jesus was like, we have a plethora of eye witness accounts and stories and deep reflections on him from those who walked with him as well as further writings from those who followed him within a short time after his ascension. We also have an assurance that Jesus *faithfully* reflects the personality and character of God to us. Thirdly, we have the assurance of our own personal encounters with Jesus as evidence and proof of what he is really like.

If we want to know what God is like, we can see him in the life and ministry of the Second Person of the Trinity very clearly.

Eyewitness accounts and biblical narrative

His faithfulness to the actual character and heart of God

Personal encounter and his power at work in our lives today

Eyewitness accounts and biblical narrative

The New Testament is an accurate and reliable account of the life and ministry of Jesus of Nazareth. Despite the fact that there is an increased tendency to try and dismiss parts of the story of Jesus' life and impact in many parts of the church's life today, we are told in the Bible itself that the stories it recounts are reliable and trustworthy:[88]

Since many have undertaken to set down an orderly account of the events that have been fulfilled among us, just as they were handed on to us by those who from the beginning were eyewitnesses and servants of the word, I too decided, after investigating everything carefully from the very first, to write an orderly account for you, most excellent Theophilus, so that you may know the truth concerning the things about which you have been instructed.
Luke 1:1-4 (NRSV)

In the first book, Theophilus, I wrote about all that Jesus did and taught from the beginning until the day when he was taken up to heaven, after giving instructions through the Holy Spirit to the apostles, whom he had chosen. After his suffering he presented himself alive to them by many convincing proofs, appearing to them during forty days and speaking about the kingdom of God...
Acts 1:1-3 (NRSV)

You also are to testify because you have been with me from the beginning.
John 15:27 (NRSV)

Now Jesus did many other signs in the presence of his disciples, which are not written in this book. But these are written so that you may come to believe that Jesus is the Messiah, the Son of God, and that through believing you may have life in his name.
John 20:30-31 (NRSV)

This is the disciple who is testifying to these things and has written them, and we know that his testimony is true. But there are also many other things that Jesus did; if every one of them were written down, I suppose that the world itself could not contain the books that would be written.
John 21:24 (NRSV)

---

88   See also passages such as Acts 11:4; 2 Timothy 4:5,17; Mark 1:1.

...we cannot keep from speaking about what we have seen and heard...
Acts 4:20 (NRSV)

For we did not follow cleverly devised myths when we made known to you the power and coming of our Lord Jesus Christ, but we had been eyewitnesses of his majesty.
2 Peter 1:16 (NRSV)

John, to the seven churches that are in Asia: Grace to you and peace from him who is and who was and who is to come, and from the seven spirits who are before his throne, and from Jesus Christ, the faithful witness, the firstborn of the dead, and the ruler of the kings of the earth.
Revelation 1:4-5 (NRSV)

There is also a sense in the Bible of the whole story being affirmed and an invitation to the reader or the listener to engage with the Bible with an assurance that it is God's word to his people and that it is given for our own strengthening and faith building:[89]

All scripture is inspired by God and is useful for teaching, for reproof, for correction and for training in righteousness, so that everyone who belongs to God may be proficient, equipped for every good work.
2 Timothy 3:16-17 (NRSV)

You cannot help but get the feeling that the writers of the various aspects of the Bible knew that they were involved in something that was much bigger and more important than themselves. They were part of a culture that took accurate records and the passing on of information extremely seriously, and they went out of their way to ensure that what they said was an accurate reflection of what they had been told. We can, therefore, trust that the content of the Bible is reliable.

---

89   See also Romans 15:4; 2 Peter 1:20,21.

God in flesh and blood – beyond an idea[90]

The powerful story of the Gospels tells us of the actual Jesus who lived and breathed and walked in first century Israel. He is not a concept or an idea, but a person. We must not under-estimate the significance of the Incarnation. The Second Person of the Trinity came into an actual context. He had to learn to walk and sit at the table. He was taught a trade by Joseph, his earthly father. When his public ministry began, people were astonished by him and taken aback by his words, precisely because many of them still thought of him as 'the carpenter's son':

Coming to his hometown, he began teaching the people in their synagogue, and they were amazed. "Where did this man get this wisdom and these miraculous powers?" they asked. "Isn't this the carpenter's son? Isn't his mother's name Mary, and aren't his brothers James, Joseph, Simon and Judas? Aren't all his sisters with us? Where then did this man get all these things?
Matthew 13:54-56 (NIV)

At the heart of Christianity we see not just an idea of God, but a person who shows us what God is like – the Lord Jesus. His interactions with people, his struggles with temptation, his engagement with religious authorities, his practice of prayer...his example is real and tangible. He is the only figure in any religion to claim not simply to point to a way of life, but to be that way. His words about himself, evidenced in his character, his behaviour and his ministry are astounding.[91]

The concrete challenge of Jesus' life and example confronts us and inspires us on a daily basis. This was wonderfully illustrated in Charles M. Sheldon's novel, *In His Steps*, from which the famous 'What Would Jesus Do?' phrase originates.[92] The story recounts the impact of the simple decision to follow Jesus and the challenges this choice presents. A revolution is sparked in the First Church of Raymond when Rev. Henry Maxwell is confronted by a young man who has hit hard times. Here's how Sheldon describes this fictional church on the Sunday when everything began to change:

The First Church of Raymond believed in having the best music that money could buy, and its quarter choir this morning was a source of great pleasure to the congregation. The anthem was inspiring. All the music was in keeping with the subject of the sermon...[93]

As the service continues, everything is very nice and respectable until the young man, who had been to visit Rev. Maxwell just a few days before, walks to the front of the church at the end of the sermon. The visitor to the church has lost his wife and is struggling to try and get his little daughter back. The book is set in the time of the Great Depression when the suffering he is enduring was evident across American society. Referring to the message that Rev. Maxwell had just preached, the desperate young father speaks to the entire congregation, saying:

---

90   See John 1:14 in The Message paraphrase.
91   Perhaps the most famous example of this is the Lord Jesus' dramatic claim to be 'the way, the truth and the life' in his farewell discourse with his disciples. See John 14-17, but particularly his words to Thomas in John 14:6.

---

92   SHELDON, Charles M., In His Steps (Old Tappan, N.J.: Spire Books, 1972, 17th Edition, first published 1962).
93   Ibid. p. 7.

"...I was wondering as I sat there under the gallery, if what you call following Jesus is the same thing as what [Jesus] taught. What did He mean when He said: 'Follow me!'?

The minister said that it is necessary for the disciple of Jesus to follow His steps, and he said the steps are obedience, faith, love and imitation. But I did not hear him tell you just what he meant that to mean, especially the last step.

What do you Christians mean by following the steps of Jesus?...What do you mean when you sing, 'I'll go with Him, with Him all the way?' Do you mean that you are suffering and denying yourselves and trying to save lost, suffering humanity just as I understand Jesus did? What do you mean by it?

I see the ragged edge of things a good deal. I understand there are more than five hundred men in this city in my case. Most of them have families. My wife died four months ago. I'm glad she is out of trouble. My little girl is staying with a printer's family until I find a job. Somehow I get puzzled when I see so many Christians living in luxury and singing, 'Jesus, I my cross have taken, all to leave and follow Thee,' and remember how my wife died in New York City, gasping for air and asking God to take the little girl too. Of course I don't expect you people can prevent everyone from dying of starvation, lack of proper nourishment and tenement air, but what does following Jesus mean? I understand that Christian people own a good many tenements. A member of a church was the owner of the one where my wife died, and I have wondered if following Jesus all the way was true in his case...

It seems to me there's an awful lot of trouble in the world that somehow wouldn't exist at all if all the people who sing such songs went and lived them out. I suppose I don't understand. But what would Jesus do? Is that what you mean by following His steps? It seems to me sometimes as if the people in the big churches had good clothes and nice houses to live in, and money to spend for luxuries, and could go away on summer vacations and all that, while the people outside the churches, thousands of them, I mean, die in tenements, and walk the streets for jobs, and never have a piano or a picture in the house, and grow up in misery and drunkenness and sin."[94]

---

94   Ibid. pp. 11-12. Punctuation altered to ease reading.

The reality is that such a question does not need to be answered with theories or ideas or hypotheses. Jesus shows us what to do because he tangibly and evidently lived, walked and died and rose again. Perhaps the question should be 'What did Jesus do?' rather than, 'What would Jesus do?'

It is easy for us to turn our spirituality into a set of 'what ifs' and 'maybes' and 'perhaps I coulds' but the clear, evident and uncomfortable reality for us is that the Incarnation does not give us such an option. If following Jesus does not look like the tangible Jesus, then how on earth can we claim to be following him at all?

Three people who were convinced by the story of Scripture

There have been many people who have sought to prove that the story of Jesus as recorded in the Bible was inaccurate. Three such people were Frank Morison, Lee Strobel and Josh McDowell. They each tell their own story.

Frank Morison was a lawyer who wrote his book, Who Moved The Stone? and first published it in 1930. He was convinced that the story of the resurrection wasn't true, but as he studied it, he realized that he was wrong. The book tells the story of how the facts of Jesus death and resurrection changed his mind. In his explanation for the book he writes:

I need not stay to describe here how, fully ten years later, the opportunity came to study the life of Christ as I had long wanted to study it, to investigate the origins of its literature, to sift some of the evidence at first hand, and to form my own judgment on the problem which it presents. I will only say that it effected a revolution in my thought. Things emerged from that old-world story which previously I should have thought impossible. Slowly, but very definitely, the conviction grew that the drama of those unforgettable weeks of human history was stranger and deeper than it seemed. It was the strangeness of many notable things in the story which first arrested and held my interest. It was only later that the irresistible logic of their meaning came into view.[95]

Josh McDowell wrote *Evidence that Demands a Verdict* in 1972. He has written a number of additions to the book since then. He, similarly, set out to disprove the story of Christ's life, death and resurrection. He wrote:

---

95   MORISON, Frank, Who Moved The Stone? (London: Faber, 1958), pp. 11,12.

Is the Bible historically reliable? Is there credible evidence of Christ's claim to be God? Will Christianity stand up before 21st Century critics? Yes.[96]

Lee Strobel wrote *The Case for Christ* in 1998.[97] He approached the story as a journalist, using all his research skills to find its flaws, but discovered that the biblical account held true. In a later book, entitled *The Case for Faith*, he wrote this:

To be honest, I didn't want to believe that Christianity could radically transform someone's character and values. It was much easier to raise doubts and manufacture outrageous objections that to consider the possibility that God actually could trigger a revolutionary turn-around in such a depraved and degenerate life.[98]

Each of these men changed their minds about Jesus after they had read the Bible. Many years ago, I came very close to ignoring large parts of the Old Testament and changing the meaning of the bits that I really disagreed with. I realized, however, that Jesus never apologized for his Father or for the Hebrew Scriptures, and therefore I did not need to. In a moment, I made a decision that I would submit myself to God's Word, and that even when I struggled with it and found it hard to accept, I would put its teaching above my own assumptions. In other words, I would submit to it in faith, even when I did not understand it, because I believe it to be more reliable and true than my own judgement. When my morality and ethics clash with the Bible's, it is because I am fallen and my judgement is wrong at worst and partial at best.

96   MCDOWELL, Josh, Evidence That Demands A Verdict (San Bernadino, Here's Life Publishers, 1972).
97   STROBEL, Lee, The Case For Christ: A Journalist's Personal Investigation Of The Evidence for Jesus (Grand Rapids: Zondervan, 1998).
98   STROBEL, Lee, The Case For Faith: A Journalist Investigates The Toughest Objections To Christianity (Grand Rapids: Zondervan, 2000).

- When was the last time your reading of the Bible caused you to change your mind about something?

- What do you think is the difference between coming to the Bible to prove a point and coming to the Bible to ask a question with an open mind?

- Can you think of issues or situations, where you have come to the Bible to justify your already held view, rather than asking God to clearly guide you through your reading of Scripture?

- What aspects of Jesus' life and ministry do you find the hardest to believe or accept? How can reading the Bible from a position of faith and trust help you with that?

His faithfulness to the actual character and heart of God.

The second aspect of the 'tangible' nature of the Lord Jesus is that he accurately reflects what God is like to us.

The Incarnation is not a last ditch attempt to show us God, it is a full revelation of what God is *actually* like. In it, we see hitherto hidden or only partially revealed aspects of God's character and heart clearly shown.

This is surely one of the most powerful and challenging aspects of the ministry and purpose of God's Son for us. He comes to us, whilst we are still fallen and lost.[99] He shows us what God is like.[100] He reveals God's heart to us.[101] He mixes and mingles with people whom Israel has shunned and ostracized up to this point.[102] He tells his disciples that when they have seen him, they have seen the Father.[103] He speaks of God in intimate and personal ways that would have shocked and angered the Pharisees and the Scribes.[104] He forgives sins,[105] he accepts worship,[106] he claims ultimate authority.[107] He speaks of God in ways that Israel has never heard before.[108]

There is perhaps no clearer articulation of this sense of Jesus *authentically* and *comprehensively* representing God to us than in the words Paul uses to the believers in Colossae. In his short letter to this fledgling Church, Paul emphasizes again and again that in Christ, they see what God is really like:[109]

He is the image of the invisible God, the firstborn of all creation; for in him all things in heaven and on earth were created, things visible and invisible, whether thrones or dominions or rulers or powers – all things have been created through him and for him. He himself is before all things and in him all things hold together. He is the head of the body, the church; he is the beginning, the firstborn from the dead, so that he might come to have first place in everything. For in him all the fullness of God was pleased to dwell, and through him God was pleased to reconcile to himself all things, whether on earth or in heaven, by making peace through the blood of his cross.
Colossians 1:15-20 (NRSV)

Let Jesus be who he claimed to be

So as we look at Christ, we see what God is really like. We must be careful, however to let him speak for himself, rather than putting words into his mouth. Jesus asked his own disciples who the people around them thought that Jesus was, and then he asked them directly as his followers who they thought he was.[110] Some thought he was a prophet, some thought he was Elijah brought back to life, others thought he was a mysterious figure. Peter answered Jesus' question directly:

YOU ARE THE CHRIST, THE SON OF THE LIVING GOD.
Matthew 16:16 (NRSV)

---

99   See Romans 5.
100   See Colossians 1.
101   See John 17:25-27.
102   See Luke 15.
103   See John 14.
104   See Matthew 6.
105   See Luke 5.
106   See Matthew 14:33 & John 9:38, for example.
107   See Matthew 28:16ff.
108   See the 'I am' sayings of John's Gospel, in particular John 6:35; 8:12; 10:9,11; 11:25; 14:6; 15:1.
109   See also Colossians 1:27; 2:2-5, 6-15; 3:1-4.

110   See Matthew 16.

Despite protestations to the contrary, Jesus' claims for himself were profound and challenging, not just for his own day, but for ours. There are implicit claims in his public life and ministry that he is divine.

- He claims to be the Messiah, or the Deliverer of Israel.[111]

- He describes himself as the Son of God.[112]

- He equates himself to God when the devil tempts him.[113]

- He asserts that he has greater authority than Moses and attributes the voice and authority of God to his own words.[114]

- He equates his 'Lordship' with God's.[115]

- He forgives sin – only God can do that.[116]

- He describes himself as Lord of the Sabbath[117] and therefore Lord of the 'Law'.

- He promises that where two or three gather in his name, he will be there – a claim to omnipresence, he also promises never to leave his disciples.[118]

- He describes himself as 'Lord'.[119]

- He acknowledges that he is 'the Son of God'.[120]

- He uses the intimate word 'Abba' for his Father.[121]

- Luke reports Jesus instructing a man to tell all that God had done for him.[122]

- Jesus attributes himself as God when the one leper returns to thank him for healing.[123]

- Jesus clearly identifies himself with the Messiah on his entry to Jerusalem.[124]

- Jesus clearly equates himself with God to the extent that the Jews are outraged.[125]

111   See John 4; John 10:22-42.
112   See John 10:36.
113   See Matthew 4:7; Luke 4:12.
114   See Matthew 5:21-11; 27-28; 31-32; 33-34; 38-39; 43-44.
115   See Matthew 7:21-22; Luke 6:46.
116   See Matthew 9:2; Mark 2:5; Luke 5:20; Luke 7:48.
117   See Matthew 12:8; Mark 2:28; Luke 6:5.
118   See Matthew 18:20; 28:16-20.
119   See Matthew 21:3; Luke 19:31,34.
120   See Matthew 26:64; Mark 14:62; Luke 22:70.
121   See Mark 14:36.
122   See Luke 8:39.
123   See Luke 17:18.
124   See Luke 19:38,40.
125   See John 5, particularly v. 18. The claims of this chapter are profuse and profound – see vv. 21-22, 23. John's Gospel is replete with profound claims by Christ – see the 'I am' sayings as noted elsewhere, but also see John 6:38; 8:19,23,58; John 10:18,30,36,38; 12:45; 13:13; 14:10,28; 16:15,28; 17:5,24; 20:17. Also see His extraordinary personal claims in Revelation 1:17 (cf. Is 41:4; 44:6; 48:12); 2:8.

You cannot read the New Testament in any depth without realizing that Jesus makes the boldest and most audacious claim imaginable to the audience around him. He is no less than God who has come to them, to reach out the hand of hope and friendship. He is the King who has come to establish his Kingdom. He is the Messiah who has come to deliver his people. He is the Son of God, the Son of Man. He is the One who brings life, hope and deliverance with him. He is to be worshipped, adored and followed. Yet he comes as a carpenter, with no great possessions.

Can anything good come from Nazareth?

He comes from Nazareth, a place that very little good had come from previously.[126]

It may be that people still look at Christianity, and at the One whom Christians follow, and disdainfully ask, 'Can anything good come from Nazareth?' The reality is, of course, that it is in this One from Nazareth that we see all Goodness. Christianity still offers the world an encounter with the One True God.

How good are we at letting Jesus speak for himself?

Personal encounter and his power at work in our lives today

The third aspect of the tangible power of Jesus is the impact that he has made in the millions and millions of people who have followed him across the world. There is something quite remarkable about the power of God working through the life and example of Jesus, to change lives.

The Bible itself is full of stories of lives transformed by an encounter with Jesus. From those he called to follow him[127] to those he healed and delivered[128], every page of the Gospels overflows with the life-changing power of Jesus tangibly evidenced in people's lives.[129]

In his book *Encounters with Jesus*, Tim Keller speaks of the power of Jesus' encounters with people and the way it has impacted Keller's own life and ministry:

I still accept the authority of all of the Bible, and love learning and teaching from all of it. But I first felt the personal weight of the Bible's spiritual authority in the Gospels, particularly in those conversations Jesus had with individuals...I suppose you could say that many of my own formative encounters with Jesus came from studying his encounters with individuals in the Gospels.[130]

The church that I lead is full of people who have been changed by the power and the grace of God as seen and encountered through Jesus. Any local church has people whose whole destiny and understanding has been transformed by an encounter with Jesus.

Jesus Christ is still tangibly and powerfully transforming lives today. He has changed my life. He may well have changed yours. He is still present in the world through his people, and he now calls us to be his hands and feet in our workplaces, our homes, our schools, our universities and our communities. His tangible power is at work across generations, cultures and societies.

Bilquis Sheikh recounts the story of her conversion from Islam to Christianity in her book, *I Dared to Call Him Father*. She speaks of the power of encountering Jesus and the truth of who he is.

---

126   See Nathaniel's words in John 1:46 and his disparaging question, 'Can anything good come from Nazareth?'

127   For example, see the powerful call 'Come follow me' recorded in Matthew 4:18-21 as Jesus calls Simon Peter and his brother Andrew as well as James and his brother, John.
128   For example see the accounts of Jesus' healing power and His deliverance ministry in Matthew 8.
129   The Apostle Paul describes his ministry in terms of the power and impact of the Lord Jesus, who appeared to Paul after Jesus had been crucified and resurrected and had gone to heaven. See Acts 9, 22 and 26.
130   KELLER, Tim, Encounters With Jesus: Unexpected Answers To Life's Biggest Questions (London: Hodder and Stoughton, 2013), p. xii.

As she read the Christian Scriptures, she recalls,
Something happened to me as I went through the book; instead of reading the Bible, I found myself living it.
Bilquis Sheikh, *I Dared to Call Him Father*[131]

Catherine Campbell comes from Northern Ireland. She and her husband Philip had three children – Cheryl, Paul and Joy. Both Cheryl and Joy were born with multiple disabilities and both died. Catherine speaks movingly of her story in her book, Under The Rainbow. I have rarely read such a moving account of faith in the face of loss. It was Catherine's faith in Jesus that carried her through:

For a period of almost twenty years, God had allowed me to care for our two beautiful, brave daughters. I have never stopped being their mother; it is just that now we cannot be together for a while. They, however, continue to bless my life every day that I live. I would be lying if I said that I wouldn't have changed a thing, for what mother would deliberately choose suffering for her children?

What I wouldn't change, however, is the perspective that having Cheryl and Joy has added to my thinking. I can now value people for who they are, and not merely for what they can do. And I am utterly convinced that life here pales into insignificance in comparison with what lies ahead for those who love Christ. Neither would I have wanted to miss all that I have learned about God, and from God. It has been both priceless and precious.
Catherine Campbell, Under The Rainbow[132]

Sheridan Voysey is a speaker at Spring Harvest. He now lives in the UK but is an Australian writer and broadcaster. He and his wife Merryn are unable to have children. In his book, *Resurrection Year*, he writes hauntingly and beautifully of their journey and of how faith in Jesus has held them and strengthened them for the years ahead:
After forty years in the wilderness, the Jews entered the Promised Land. After forty days in the wilderness, Jesus launched his world-changing mission. And this gives me hope as I look out over Abingdon Road. After the wilderness comes a new beginning...
Sheridan Voysey, *Resurrection Year*[133]

Barnabas Mam has been the regional director in Asia for Ambassadors for Christ International since 2007. He is a Spring Harvest speaker and will be sharing some of his story with us. He is a Cambodian and joined the Communist party as a teenager. He was converted to Christ whilst spying on a Christian evangelistic meeting in the early 1970's. He was later arrested and sent to the Killing Fields where he spent four years in captivity. After his release, Barnabas was forced to flee the country and he spent another eight years in a refugee camp in Thailand. After returning home, Barnabas helped rebuild the church in Cambodia, and he has been involved in planting over 400 churches since. In his book, *Church Behind the Wire*, he writes this of a conversation he had with his father, who was a Buddhist, about Barnabas' own newfound faith in Christ:

Dad, just like I've said before; Jesus is in my heart. I can worship Him anywhere. If everything is taken away, I will worship Him on the back of a water buffalo. I will worship Him in the branches of a tree. I will worship Him while rowing a boat. He is everywhere.
Barnabas Mam, *Church Behind the Wire*[134]

We do not need to look very far to see the tangible evidence of Jesus. Perhaps we only need to look at what we have become or the person sitting next to us in church.

131 SHEIKH, Bilquis, I Dared to Call Him Father: An incredible journey of discovery begins when a high-born Muslim woman opens the Bible (Eastbourne: Kingsway, 1978).
132 CAMPBELL, Catherine, Under the Rainbow: A Mother's Experiences of the Promises of God (Oxford: Monarch, 2008), pp. 189-190.
133 VOYSEY, Sheridan, Resurrection Year: Turning Broken Dreams into New Beginnings (Nashville: Thomas Nelson, 2013) p. 195.
134 MAM, Barnabas, Church Behind the Wire: A Story of Faith in the Killing Fields (Chicago: Moody Press, 2012) pp. 180-181.

What does 'tangible' mean in different contexts?

Across the various 'spaces' in Spring Harvest this year, the idea of God the Son being 'tangible' will have different implications, but what are the core principles that we can apply to every area of our lives? Take a look at the diagram below and think about the answers to the questions for the 'space' you are in.

Principle 1
Jesus is reliable

Principle 2
Jesus shows us what God is like

Principle 3
Jesus is still able to change lives and situations

Principle 4
The power of Jesus looks like something in my situation

Principle 5
My words and my story can convey Jesus to those around me

Jesus working through his Church is a tangible expression of his love and power

We can often think only of the church 'gathered' as the model of our life and witness, and if we are not careful, we can narrow ministry down to what we do in the name of a local congregation or a Christian organization – but what if the Second Person of the Trinity wants to work through you in your workplace and your home? What if the Gospel of Christ impacts every area of your life – everything you say and everything you do? What if Christ wants to be seen and heard and touched through you?

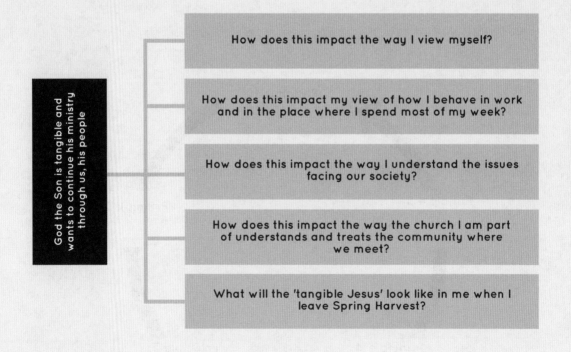

God the Son is tangible and wants to continue his ministry through us, his people

How does this impact the way I view myself?

How does this impact my view of how I behave in work and in the place where I spend most of my week?

How does this impact the way I understand the issues facing our society?

How does this impact the way the church I am part of understands and treats the community where we meet?

What will the 'tangible Jesus' look like in me when I leave Spring Harvest?

Further questions for personal reflection or group discussion:

What do you think are the implications of treating Jesus like an 'idea' rather than a person?

In what ways do you think you can let God live through you, as he lived through Jesus? Are there particular areas of your life and faith that you find very hard to let God use? How can that change?

Think of ways that you could 'be Jesus' in situations you are facing at work or at home. Don't worry about 'feeling' good about it, just make a decision to do what Jesus would do.

Think about creating a small group that would meet once a week to ask the same simple question that was asked by the small group in Charles Sheldon's book, In *His Steps*. Could you try it for a month at Advent or Christmas? Meet once a week and discuss the choices you have made under the simple but beautiful challenge: What would Jesus do?

Lessons from the Methodist Covenant Prayer

The Methodist Church has a beautiful tradition in which, once a year, the members of a local congregation make a covenant with one another. The 'Methodist Covenant Prayer' is included below. As you contemplate the image of surrender here, pray these words slowly and intentionally. Maybe you could do this as a community or as a family or with an accountability partner? Or maybe you could pray this with someone you are with this week as a sign of what God is doing in your heart and life.

I am no longer my own but yours.
Put me to what you will,
rank me with whom you will;
put me to doing, put me to suffering;
let me be employed for you
or laid aside for you,
exalted for you or brought low for you.
Let me be full, let me be empty,
let me have all things,
let me have nothing.
I freely and wholeheartedly
yield all things
to your pleasure and disposal.
And now, glorious and blessed God,
Father, Son and Holy Spirit,
you are mine and I am yours.
So be it.
And the covenant made on earth,
let it be ratified in heaven.
Amen.

God the Son is tender

We do not only believe that God the Son is tangible, we also believe that he is tender. The Apostles' Creed does not only root Jesus in time and history, it also shows us the purpose of his life and ministry:

I believe in Jesus Christ, his only Son, our Lord.
Who was conceived by the Holy Spirit,
born of the Virgin Mary,
suffered under Pontius Pilate,
was crucified, died, and was buried;
He descended to the dead.

Jesus is 'tender' in a number of ways.

- He is tender for us because he lived for us, was bruised and broken for us and endured great pain for us.

- He is tender towards us because he is patient and kind with us.

Tender 'for' us

One of the greatest and profoundest mysteries of the Christian faith is the reality that Jesus endured pain for us and died for us. He endured great limitation for us.[135] It is impossible to explain this properly. All of our words ultimately fail to convey the reality of God's willingness to limit himself in order to reach us. Indeed, all the words in the world could not explain it. John tried to explain the beauty and the life of Jesus in his Gospel, and you can almost sense his confession that he just can't do it in the closing words of his beautiful book:

This is the disciple who is testifying to these things and has written them, and we know that his testimony is true. But there are also many other things that Jesus did; if every one of them were written down, I suppose that the world itself could not contain the books that would be written.
John 21:24-25 (NRSV)

Jesus was limited in knowledge[136] and had to grow up like any other boy. He endured thirst and hunger. He was ridiculed, misunderstood and mocked.[137] He was falsely accused and abandoned.[138] Ultimately, he was beaten and murdered.[139] Why?

---

135   See Philippians 2 and its powerful description of Jesus' self-limitation for us.
136   See Luke 2:40.
137   See Isaiah 53 and John 18-20.
138   See Luke 22:47–23:43.
139   See Matthew 27:45-56.

The mystery of his suffering may be complex and layered, but the reasons for it are simple. He did it for love. Perhaps the most well-known verse in the Bible captures it most beautifully:

For God so loved the world that he gave his only Son, so that everyone who believes in him may not perish but may have eternal life.
John 3:16 (NRSV)

The New Testament is replete with passages that speak of Christ's love being the driving force behind his sacrifice for us.[140] I find it a powerful idea that the first words spoken about Jesus in his public ministry refer to him taking away the sins of the world[141] and some of his last recorded words echo this cry for forgiveness.[142] Christ's atoning sacrifice for our sins[143] and his willingness to bear the brunt of our punishment[144] and pay the ransom for our sins[145] demonstrate a tenderness and compassion that goes beyond description. A tenderness so great is shared between the Father and the Son that the Son is willing to endure the wrath of the Father for our forgiveness, and even though it must have broken the hearts of both the Father and the Son, they were willing to carry that pain for our redemption.

Tenderness 'towards' us

Yet it is not only in his suffering and death that we see his tenderness. It is in his whole life and ministry. One of the great challenges that faces many Christians is that they do not know what to do with the life and ministry of Jesus. They celebrate his birth and his death, but end up fumbling around with his life. Jesus' love and tenderness for us is not only demonstrated in his being incarnated and

being crucified, it is also demonstrated in the whole of his life and ministry: he welcomed children,[146] he embraced and celebrated the role of women,[147] he welcomed the outcasts (as I mentioned earlier), he spoke tenderly to the grieving[148] and he looked into the eyes of the poor and the destitute and treated them with dignity.[149] His tenderness got him into trouble with the religious authorities, but it also gave people hope.[150]

It is this tenderness that still gives people hope today. Many people think that God is against them, that he delights in punishing them, rejecting them and subjecting them to terrible pain and suffering. This is often not helped by angry preachers and over-zealous evangelists who try to force people into the Kingdom. Do not misunderstand me, Jesus could be zealous and direct when he wanted to be. He cast the money lenders out of the Temple[151] and he was clear in his condemnation of religious legalists,[152] but he was also tender and gentle and kind. He knelt beside the woman taken in adultery,[153] he went out of his way to talk to a woman at a well,[154] he wept over the death of his friend and the grief of Mary and Martha,[155] as well as over Jerusalem as its people rejected him.[156]

Brennan Manning was captivated by the tenderness of Jesus. He once said that his deepest awareness of himself was that he was deeply loved by Jesus Christ and that he had done nothing to earn it or deserve it. His words taught me to understand that I should define myself as someone who is radically loved by God because everything

---

140   It is almost impossible to give verses for reflection on this theme without looking at the whole of the New Testament. Reading the prayers of Paul for the Ephesian church recorded in Ephesians 1:15-23 and Ephesians 3:14-21 helps you to capture something of the yearning of a pastor for people to understand just how much Christ loves them.
141   See John 1:29.
142   See Luke 23:34.
143   See 1 John 2:2.
144   See 1 Peter 2:24.
145   See Mark 10:45.

146   See Matthew 19:13-15.
147   I love the description of Jesus allowing Mary to sit at His feet in Luke 10. This was a position that only men would normally be given and in his actions, Jesus is not only embracing Mary, he is embracing all women to come and sit at His feet, equal to any man.
148   See Jesus' exchange with the widow of Nain recorded in Luke 7:11-17.
149   See the Sermon on the Mount in Matthew 5-7 or the Sermon on the Plain in Luke 6.
150   See Matthew 7:28-29 for the positive and amazed response of ordinary people, and John 5:16 for the response of the religious leaders because Jesus was challenging their position and power.
151   See Matthew 21.
152   See Matthew 23.
153   See John 8.
154   See John 4.
155   See John 11.
156   See Luke 19:41-44.

else is an illusion. He explores the tenderness of Jesus in his book, *The Lion And Lamb*. The book is a powerful and beautiful call to return to the tender yet transforming power of the Lord Jesus. In it, Manning aches for Christians to love more, because Christ loved so much:

Our Life in Christ. It's not an easy thing to grasp. Maybe you understand it only by living it. And maybe Augustine was right on the money when he wrote: "Give me someone who loves and he will understand what I am trying to say. Give me someone whose heart yearns, who feels the nostalgia of loneliness in exile, who is athirst and sighs for the fatherland eternal, give me such a one and he will understand what I am trying to say. But if I must explain myself to ice-cold indifference, he will not understand."[157]

My brothers and sisters, Jesus is our God. He and the Father are one. He is the image of the invisible God. Our Jesus image makes all the difference. If we let the Lion of Judah run loose as Lord of our lives, He will not want us to be poor, broken, or sad. Yet He may allow it, knowing that in these conditions we are more likely to let Him make us rich, whole, and happy.[158]

I wonder what would happen if we allowed the tenderness of Christ to be heard in our words and seen in our eyes? Perhaps the world around us would pay more attention to us if we paid more attention to it? Perhaps it would listen more to us if we first stopped and listened to the pain in its heart or we took the time to see the beauty in the world, not just the ugliness?

Tender Jesus,
Help me to see the world through your eyes.
Give me grace to look beyond my own narrow judgements.
Help me to listen more and speak less.
Help me to understand more and judge less harshly.
Help me to stoop down and kneel beside those I see.
Help me not to write others off.

Tender Jesus,
You have dealt tenderly with me – thank you.
You look beyond my failings – thank you.
You listen to me – thank you.
Your judgement is pure and you understand me perfectly – thank you.
You stooped down and knelt before me – thank you.
You have not written me off – thank you.

Tender Jesus,
Forgive us when we lose sight of your tenderness.
Restore to us the gentleness that comes from spending time with you.
Shine through the cracked glass of our lives
That others may find hope and grace in you as we have.

Amen.

157   MANNING, Brennan, The Lion And Lamb: The Relentless
Tenderness of Jesus (Grand Rapids: Fleming H. Revell, 1986).
158   Ibid.

The challenge of tenderness

Sometimes we run away from tenderness because we are fearful of it. We don't know how to cope with compassion and gentleness. It 'undoes' us. Yet, if we dealt tenderly with others, we might find ourselves received very differently.

Imagine that there are two basic stances you can adopt in your engagement with other people. One is a stance of attack, when you approach them with your fists up – either to fight them or to defend yourself. The other is a stance of friendship, when you offer them your hand in friendship or embrace. This idea is explored challengingly in the work and writings of Mirsolav Volf.[159] He reminds us of the need not only to know Christ's tenderness, but to share it in every aspect of our lives.

Take some time to reflect on some of your hardest relationships and challenges. Which 'posture' do you take in those situations? If it is the posture of 'attack', what can you do to change that?

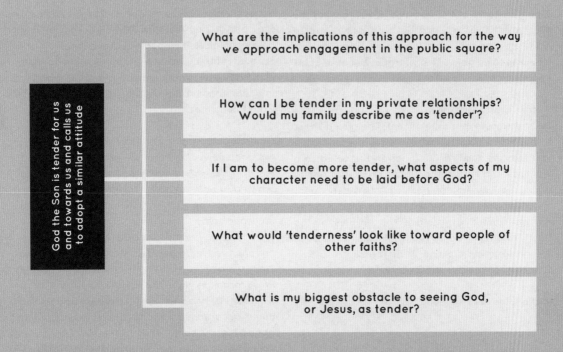

God the Son is tender for us and towards us and calls us to adopt a similar attitude

What are the implications of this approach for the way we approach engagement in the public square?

How can I be tender in my private relationships? Would my family describe me as 'tender'?

If I am to become more tender, what aspects of my character need to be laid before God?

What would 'tenderness' look like toward people of other faiths?

What is my biggest obstacle to seeing God, or Jesus, as tender?

159   VOLF, Miroslav, Exclusion and Embrace: A Theological Exploration of Identity, Otherness and Reconciliation (Nashville: Abingdon, 1996); Free of Charge: Giving and Forgiving in a Culture Stripped of Grace (Grand Rapids: Zondervan, 2005); A Public Faith: How Followers of Christ Should Serve the Common Good (Grand Rapids: Brazos Press, 2011).

God the Son is able to transform us

Returning to the Apostles' Creed for the last time in this section, we are reminded that our belief in Jesus also means we believe:

> ON THE THIRD DAY HE ROSE AGAIN;
> HE ASCENDED INTO HEAVEN,
> HE IS SEATED AT THE RIGHT HAND
> OF THE FATHER,
> AND HE WILL COME TO JUDGE
> THE LIVING AND THE DEAD.

Resurrection changes everything

Whilst this part of the Apostles' Creed covers the Ascension of Jesus[160] and his promised return to judge the world,[161] I want to explore what it means for Jesus to be able to transform us because of his resurrection.[162]

If the cross is God's 'No!' to sin, then the resurrection is his magnificent, life-giving 'Yes!' to hope and transformation. Indeed, despite the fact that the resurrection is often relegated to a few lines in a sermon about the cross, the reality is that the whole of the book of Acts is dependent upon the bold and hope-giving proclamation of the resurrected Christ, and the epistles of the New Testament would make almost no sense if the resurrection did not sit at the centre of the Church's convictions about Jesus.

In short, the resurrection changes everything.

The Epistles depend entirely on the assumption that Jesus is a living, reigning Saviour who is now the exalted head of the church, who is to be trusted, worshipped and adored, and who will some day return in power and great glory to reign as King over the earth.
Wayne Grudem, *Systematic Theology*[163]

The conviction that Jesus Christ rose from the dead three days after his cold and lifeless corpse was placed in a borrowed tomb is the lynchpin to the Christian faith. Without it, his life, his death and his words do not make sense. If he did not rise from the dead, then his teaching was a lie, his conversations were misleading at best and downright cruel at worst and his whole ministry becomes meaningless. The Apostle Paul argued that if Christ had not been risen from the dead, then we would be the most miserable (and I would suggest most misled) people on planet Earth.[164]

There has been much made of Christ's 'Lordship' in recent years – and rightly so. His claim to be Lord is as revolutionary now as it was when he walked on the earth in physical form. Yet his Lordship would be meaningless if he had not broken the power of sin and death by rising from the dead. Indeed, for Paul, the resurrection was of primary importance in understanding the Gospel. He writes this to the Corinthian church:

Now I would remind you, brothers and sisters, of the good news that I proclaimed to you, which you in turn received, in which you also stand, through which also you are being saved, if you hold firmly to the message that I proclaimed to you – unless you have come to believe in vain.

For I handed on to you as of first importance what I in turn had received: That Christ died for our sins in accordance with the scriptures, and that he was buried, and that he was raised on the third day in accordance with the scriptures, and that he appeared to Cephas, then to the twelve. Then he appeared to more than five hundred brothers and

---

160   See Acts 1.
161   For example, see Romans 1-4, but particularly 2:16 and 2 Timothy 4:1ff.
162   See John 20:1–21:25 for a powerful account of the resurrection story. The other accounts of the resurrection are found in Matthew 28:1-20; Mark 16:1-8 and Luke 24:1-53.

163   GRUDEM, Wayne, Systematic Theology: An Introduction To Biblical Doctrine (Grand Rapids: Zondervan, 1994), p. 608.
164   See 1 Corinthians 15.

sisters at one time, most of whom are still alive, though some have died. Then he appeared to James, then to all the apostles. Last of all, as to one untimely born, he appeared to me.
1 Corinthians 15:1-8 (NRSV)

It is impossible to read the Apostle Paul without coming to the conclusion that the resurrection of Jesus Christ lay at the heart of his understanding of his faith. There is no way of understanding the Kingdom of God, the power of forgiveness, life after death, hope, transformation or anything else within New Testament faith without the resurrection sitting at the heart of the story. Indeed, the life of Jesus without the resurrection of Jesus would be a wonderful moral example, but it would not fundamentally give us hope. The death of Jesus without the resurrection of Jesus would not lift our fear of death and it would not give us the assurance that our sin was destroyed forever. And it goes without saying that the life of the Spirit, the intercessory ministry of Jesus now and his promised return would be meaningless and impossible if he had not risen from the dead.

Indeed, Thomas Merton, a Trappist monk, once said that it is of the very essence of Christianity to face suffering and death not because they are good, not because they have meaning, but because the resurrection of Jesus has robbed them of their meaning.

What good would the ministry of the Second Person of the Trinity be if he were tangible and tender, but not able to transform us and the world in which we live?

Just how powerful is the 'transforming power' of God the Son?

The resurrection of Jesus does not simply affect us as individuals,[165] although it certainly does that, but it also changes the future of the entire planet. It is the first sign of the ushering in of a brand new Kingdom that will never end.[166] Indeed, Paul tells us that the whole creation 'groans and yearns' for the power of the resurrected Christ to transform it.[167]

The Apostle John paints the resurrection story as a New Creation story in his Gospel. Remember that Creation begins in a 'garden' in Genesis 1 and the New Creation will be consummated when the world becomes a garden city, according to the imagery of the book of Revelation (also written by John). It is surely not a coincidence, therefore, that in John 20, we see resurrection taking place in a garden and Jesus appearing to Mary as a gardener!

---

165   The personal implications of resurrection are often picked up in the symbolism of believers' baptism, where the water signifies a grave and the candidate is plunged into the 'grave' and then raised out of the water to 'new life' having identified themselves with the church of Christ and declared their allegiance to Jesus. See, for example, Romans 6.
166   See Isaiah 9:7 and Luke 1:33ff.
167   See Romans 8.

The implications of John's account are clear. It is in the moment of resurrection that life springs out of death and light springs out of darkness. This is the moment the world has been waiting for. That is why all of the epistles and the entire understanding of the New Testament concept of hope and life and victory rests in resurrection. It is because in resurrection we see the absolute power of Jesus Christ to save, rescue and transform us, our culture and the very ground upon which we stand and the planet on which we live. There are three key areas we can briefly explore to help us understand the power of transformation that the resurrection of Jesus displays:

1. **It transforms people.**[168]
2. **It transforms the planet.**[169]
3. **It transforms our purpose.**[170]

There are also three key ways in which resurrection brings transformation:

1. **It conquers Satan and evil.**[171]
2. **It removes the fear of death.**[172]
3. **It instils a new sense of hope and 're-creation'.**[173]

When you put these two things together – the power of resurrection and the ways in which resurrection brings transformation – you end up with a helpful and inspiring range of implications of the resurrection.

Resurrection	Conquers Satan and evil	Removes the fear of death	Instils a new sense of hope and re-creation
Transforms people	Releases us from the grip of an old lifestyle and wrong identity and enables us to be free and become what God created us to be.	Enables us to face death and dying with a new confidence because we know that death does not have the final word in our lives.	Gives us a new purpose – one in which we know that we will be delivered from the very presence of sin eventually.
Transforms the planet	Reverses the devastation of the Fall on the created order and removes a selfish abuse of the planet, but also reverses the deep schism caused by fallenness.	Enables the planet to be renewed and restored and once again the context of beauty, peace and blessing God intended it to be.	Lifts the sense of the created world being doomed to destruction and instead uses it as a seed for a new and perfected world.
Transforms our purpose	We are no longer caught in the grip of selfish desires but are able to stand for justice, peace and righteousness.	Our cynicism is destroyed because we know that God's purposes will be accomplished and the whole sphere of sin and death will eventually be removed, not only from us, but from the world.	We become co-workers with God in the transformation of systems, structures and the planet itself.

168   This idea is picked up in Paul's letter to the Ephesians, particularly chapter 2.
169   This idea is picked up in both Romans 8 and the beautiful pictures of new creation in the book of Revelation, particularly chapter 21.
170   Paul's words in Galatians 2:20 are a powerful example of this, "I no longer live, but Christ lives in me" – this can only be the resurrected Christ.
171   See John 10:10 and 1 John 3:8.
172   See 1 Corinthians 15.
173   See 2 Corinthians 5:17.

Transformation at every level

Thus, resurrection has a deep impact upon our understanding of ourselves and our place in the world. We become people governed by hope and not by despair. Our outlook is changed from being cyclical to being linear, because we know that history has a beginning, a middle and an end. And our motivation is no longer fear of a punishing God, but trust in a God who has rescued us and transformed us.

When Jesus announced his ministry in the synagogue in Nazareth[174] he quoted from the Prophet Isaiah.[175] He declared that he had come to 'bring good news to the poor,' and to 'proclaim release to the captives' and 'recovery of sight for the blind,' and 'to let the oppressed go free,' and 'to proclaim the year of the Lord's favour'. This powerful manifesto is seen in his whole life, sealed by his death and vindicated by his resurrection. For the Good News of Christ to be good news at all, it must be good news at every level for all who will respond to it. Only the resurrection of Christ can offer physical, social, spiritual and emotional transformation.

It reaches into the darkest places of our lives, our communities and our world and offers hope. It changes our motivation and lifts our eyes.

It changes everything.

174   See Luke 4:16.
175   See Isaiah 61.

Letting the transforming power of the Son change our perspective on ourselves and our world

We can make the Gospel too small. We can turn it into not much more than a pietistic panacea that makes us feel better about ourselves but does not challenge us to engage in the world, or we can make it into nothing more than a social mandate which makes us little more than glorified politicians or social workers. What if the transforming power of the Son forces us to play our part in changing the world, precisely because the same transforming power of the Son first changes us? What if the inevitable consequence of a genuine encounter with God the Son is that we are pushed into the world so that we can display his power to those around us?

Imagine that poverty has five faces – listed below. What does the transforming power of the Son look like in each one?

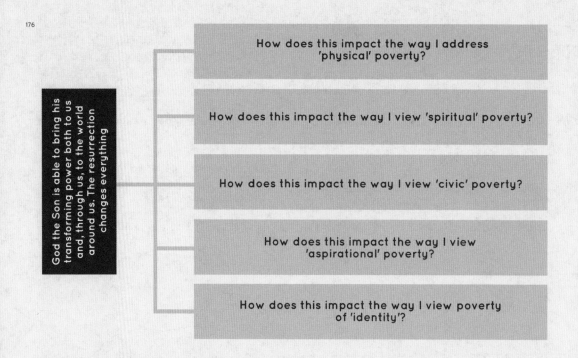

176

God the Son is able to bring his transforming power both to us and, through us, to the world around us. The resurrection changes everything

How does this impact the way I address 'physical' poverty?

How does this impact the way I view 'spiritual' poverty?

How does this impact the way I view 'civic' poverty?

How does this impact the way I view 'aspirational' poverty?

How does this impact the way I view poverty of 'identity'?

---

176   Physical poverty is a lack of material provision of some kind. Spiritual poverty is a lack of meaning and purpose. Civic poverty is a feeling of powerlessness and loss of one's place in a community or society. Aspirational poverty is a lack of dreams or ambitions or a feeling of entrapment and helplessness. Poverty of identity is a lack of worth or value in oneself. The first three of these are widely recognised by sociologists as 'categories' of poverty. The last two are additions to poverty 'categories' that I developed some years ago in relation to life in urban Britain, and the impact of what I would describe as an 'orphaned' or 'stranded' generation, who have been stripped of the moral and spiritual framework that existed in Britain more clearly before the First World War.

Further questions for personal reflection or group discussion:

How can we engage in a transforming approach to the workplace which celebrates the power and truth of resurrection?

What does a 'transformed' and 'resurrection-rooted' attitude toward the created order demand of us and enable in us?

In what ways can we engage in the world of public discussion and debate from a 'transformed' perspective?

What would a transformed politics look like and how could you play your part in it?

What are the key faces of poverty in your community and how can your church address them hopefully?

WITHOUT HIM, WE CAN DO NOTHING

ALL HAIL THE POWER OF JESUS' NAME LET ANGELS PROSTRATE FALL BRING FORTH THE ROYAL DIADEM AND CROWN HIM, CROWN HIM, CROWN HIM CROWN HIM LORD OF ALL.

Edward Perronet[177]

Each evening, during our Celebrations, we will be inviting you to go beyond 'studying' the issue we have been facing each day and to enter into an encounter with God. To do that, we will be using Jesus' powerful words of hope, comfort and challenge to his disciples contained in his parting address to them. This is known as The Farewell Discourse and is found in the Gospel of John in chapters 14-17. We will also be using Psalm 46 to help us encounter God.

Why not take a few moments either before or after the Evening Celebration, to reflect on the words of both of these passages and to ask God to either prepare you for what he wants to do in your life and heart or to confirm what he has done as you prepare to sleep.

This evening, as we focus on the reality that without Jesus, we can do nothing, we will be exploring the Farewell Discourse again, as well as Psalm 46:8-11. As you reflect on what the Lord has done in your life and heart today, take a few moments to meditate upon Psalm 46:8-11 from whatever version of the Bible you normally use.

- Are there ways in which you are guilty of trying to do things without Jesus?

- If he was to gently lift his presence from you, do you think you would notice? If you would notice, what would be the difference?

- Tonight, how can you go beyond studying and discussing Jesus to actually meeting him afresh and renewing your friendship and intimacy with him?

- Consider writing a letter or a brief message to Jesus, sharing your heart with him.

- What do you need God to do in your life tonight and how will you make space and time for him to do it?

---

177   From the hymn 'All Hail The Power Of Jesus Name' by Edward Perronet. Music by John Rippon. Normally sung to the tune, 'Coronation'.

Lord Jesus,

I so often rush into my day, asking you to bless what I am doing.
Forgive me and help me to do what you are blessing instead.
Give me the grace to see the beauty of the people you have
placed around me.

Lift my eyes to you once again.
Let me know again the freshness of your company and the
gentleness of your grace.
Slow me down enough to enable me to see you
in the most unexpected of places.

Without you I can do nothing.
Nothing I can do is worth anything without you.
Without you, anything I do is nothing.
Everything without you is still nothing.
You are everything.

Draw me to yourself again and use my life for your glory.

Amen.

The Unstoppable Spirit

The Big Start
"The Spirit who gives us strength."

Bible Study
"I believe in the Holy Spirit..."

Celebrations
Come, Holy Spirit

The Unstoppable Spirit

"His Spirit joins with our spirit to affirm that we are his children."

Romans 8:15 (NLT)

Spaces and Seminars
The God who empowers us tranforms us. He is both intimate and involved

THE SPIRIT WHO GIVES US STRENGTH

This morning in the Big Start we'll be exploring the fact that God gives us strength to face every situation. There are times when we can feel very weak, but as we turn to God, he helps us, nourishes us, protects us and empowers us. We will be exploring the amazing things that took place when Jesus was baptised, so why not read this passage before you come along to the Big Start and ask God to speak to you very clearly today?

Then Jesus went from Galilee to the Jordan River to be baptized by John. But John tried to talk him out of it. "I am the one who needs to be baptized by you," he said, "so why are you coming to me?" But Jesus said, "It should be done, for we must carry out all that God requires." So John agreed to baptize him. After his baptism, as Jesus came up out of the water, the heavens were opened and he saw the Spirit of God descending like a dove and settling on him. And a voice from heaven said, "This is my dearly loved Son, who brings me great joy.
Matthew 3:13-17 (NLT)

The Spirit and the Bride say, 'Come'

There is a beautiful invitation at the very end of the Bible where we are invited to come and meet with God: "The Spirit and the Bride say, 'Come'".[178] We can, so very often, seek our fulfilment and our strength in the wrong things: in people's affirmations of us, in compliments, in our looks, in our position, in our titles and roles. All of these will fade or change, but God's invitation is always there for those who love him and want to serve him.

We need the Holy Spirit to strengthen us about as often as we need to breathe! Try going for an hour without breathing and you'll be dead. Yet we often try to live without the constant power and presence of the Spirit.

Take a few moments today to ask God to give you strength. Maybe you can deliberately focus on your breathing and listen to it. Ask God to remind you of your constant need of him today. Breathe deeply and reflect on these words from a song by John Michael Talbot called 'Breathe':

Breathe in the Spirit of God
With each breath you take
Breathe out
All that's not of God
Breathe out
Your pain

Breathe in the Spirit of Christ
The life of Jesus
Breathe out
All that's not like Him
Breathe out your sin

Breathe in
The wind of God
Let go of your pride
Breathe out
Your old self
In Him
Yourself you'll find
John Michael Talbot, '*Breathe*'[179]

---

179   'Breathe' by John Michael Talbot is taken from his 2011 album, 'Worship And Bow Down'.

WE BELIEVE IN THE HOLY SPIRIT

The Bible study today will explore the last section of the Apostles' Creed[180]:

> I BELIEVE IN THE HOLY SPIRIT,
> THE HOLY CATHOLIC CHURCH,
> THE COMMUNION OF SAINTS,
> THE FORGIVENESS OF SINS,
> THE RESURRECTION OF THE BODY,
> AND THE LIFE EVERLASTING.

There are many Christians who have difficulties with this part of the Apostles' Creed. Sometimes they disconnect the 'I believe in the Holy Spirit' from the remaining lines and end up feeling like the Creed says little about the ministry and work of the Holy Spirit. That might be true, but actually this whole section deals with the work and ministry of the Holy Spirit.

He is the one who enables the universal Church to be a church family and see Christ at work and present in one another. He is the one who enables us to remain connected. He is the one who makes real in our hearts the efficacy of the blood of Christ and the assurance of the forgiveness of our sins. It is the Spirit's power that enables us to live in resurrection and it is the Spirit's power that gives us new (and everlasting) life!

As the Bible teachers unpack this last section of the Creed today, allow yourself to be reminded of the power and the very present reality of the person and work of the Holy Spirit. He is perhaps the most controversial aspect of God's Trinitarian character.

Many Christians try to live without him or relegate him to a place of relative obscurity. Perhaps that is because it is hard to imagine him. Tom Smail describes him in his book, *The Giving Gift*,[181] as a person without a face. Could that be why we struggle with encountering the Holy Spirit? Whatever the reason might be, may we each know his grace and strength at work in our lives today.

---

180   The role and power of the Spirit can be explored in the Bible by reading Genesis 1:1; Ezekiel 36; Joel 2:28; Acts 2; John 3, 16; Romans 8; Colossians 3 and Revelation 22 amongst other scriptures.

181   SMAIL, Tom, The Giving Gift: The Holy Spirit In Person (London: Darton, Longman and Todd, 1994)

The God who empowers us transforms us

Gordon Fee on the person and work of the Holy Spirit:

The crucial role of the Spirit in Paul's life...as the dynamic, experiential reality of Christian life – is often either overlooked or given mere lip service... I am equally convinced that the Spirit in Paul's experience and theology was always thought of in terms of the personal presence of God. The Spirit is God's way of being present, powerfully present, in our lives and communities as we await the consummation of the kingdom of God. Precisely because he understood the Spirit as God's personal presence, Paul also understood the Spirit always in terms of an empowering presence; whatever else, for Paul the Spirit was an experienced reality.[182]

182   FEE, Gordon D., God's Empowering Presence: The Holy Spirit in The Letters of Paul (Peabody: Hendrickson Publishers Inc., 1994)

What does it mean to believe in the Holy Spirit?

Is the Holy Spirit an 'it'? Is the Holy Spirit a force? Is the Holy Spirit a wind? It is precisely because the Spirit is so hard to pin down that he is also hard to describe. Yet if we are to have confidence in God at all, about anything, we need a deeper and more dynamic understanding of the Holy Spirit. He is a personality within the Godhead who shares attributes of eternity, existence and power with the Father and the Son. He is, because he is God, above gender, yet is never referred to in the Bible as 'she'.[183] He was present in creation[184] and is present in the last pages of the New Testament.[185] The Holy Spirit can be grieved,[186] he has a mind[187] and a voice.[188] He listens,[189] he directs[190] and he is referred to as God.[191]

In our exploration of the Holy Spirit today, how he gives us confidence and how we can have confidence in him, we want to explore two key areas of his ministry. Firstly, we want to examine the *intimacy* of the Holy Spirit and secondly, we want to explore the *involvement* of the Holy Spirit in the world.

The Spirit has many names and comes in many metaphors and forms through the course of Scripture:

- The Spirit of Life
  (Ezekiel 37:1-10; Jn 6:63; Rom 8:2)
- The Spirit of the Lord Jehovah (Isaiah 61:1-3)
- The Spirit of Holiness (Romans 1:4)
- The Oil of Gladness (Hebrews 1:9)
- The Holy Spirit of Promise (Ephesians 1:13)
- The Spirit of Jesus Christ (Phillippians 1:19)
- The Spirit (John 20:22; Genesis 2:7)
- The Spirit of the Living God
  (2 Corinthians 3:6)
- LORD (Acts 28:25 & Hebrews 3:7)
- The Spirit of Burning/Fire
  (Matthew 3:11; Isaiah 4:3-4)
- The Spirit of God (I Corinthians 3:16)
- The Spirit of Judgement (Isaiah 4:4)
- The Spirit of his Son (Galatians 4:6)
- The Spirit of Glory (1 Peter 4:14)
- God (Acts 5:3-4)
- The Spirit of God, and of Christ
  (1 Corinthians 3:16, Romans 8:9)
- The Spirit of Christ (Romans 8:9)
- The Eternal Spirit (Hebrews 9:14)
- The Spirit of Grace (Hebrews 10:29)
- The Spirit of Wisdom and Knowledge
  (Isaiah 11:2)
- The Spirit of Jehovah (Isaiah 11:2)
- The Spirit of Knowledge and the Fear of the
  Lord (Isaiah 11:2)
- The Holy Spirit (Luke 11:13)
- The Spirit of Grace and Supplication
  (Zechariah 12:10)
- The Comforter (John 14:26)
- The Spirit of Truth (John 14:17; 15:26)
- The Spirit of Jesus (Acts 16:6-7)
- The Spirit of Counsel and Might
  (Acts 1:8; 8:29; 16:6-7)

Yet there are many people who have been caught unawares by the Holy Spirit as he has swept through a church family or into a person's life. There are many Christians who are deeply fearful of the Spirit's work and ministry, there are others who are simply confused about who he is and what he does. Yet Jesus taught his disciples two pillars of truth that support all the other truths in

---

183 Masculine pronouns are used to describe the Holy Spirit despite the fact that the Greek word for 'Spirit' is a neuter word (See John 14:26; 15:26; 16:8,13). This does not, of course mean that the Spirit is a man. He is above gender, as is the Father.
184 See Genesis 1.
185 See Revelation 22.
186 See Ephesians 4:30 or Hebrews 10:29; Isaiah 63:10.
187 Romans 8:27.
188 For example, see Acts 13:2; Hebrews 3:7-10; Mark 13:11; 10:19-20; Acts 4:25; Revelation 2:7,11,29; 3:6,13,22.
189 See 1 Corinthians 2:10.
190 For example, see John 16:13.
191 See Acts 5 and the story of Ananias and Sapphira.

the Christian faith. He told his disciples that the secret of his own victorious life was his intimate union and friendship with his Father. He also told his disciples that their victory was dependent upon their ongoing connection to him, by the power of the Holy Spirit.[192] The life that Jesus lived qualified him for the death that he died and the death that he died qualifies us for the life that we live for him – and all of it is dependent upon the ongoing work and ministry of the Holy Spirit.

Not all Christians speak in tongues or use the Gifts of the Holy Spirit. Not all sing exuberant and boisterous songs, but you simply cannot be a Christian without the power of the Spirit being at work in your life.[193]

God the Holy Spirit is intimate and involved

The 'intimacy' and 'involvement' of the Holy Spirit begin in the very first pages of the Bible. In fact, it would be difficult to understand how he could be intimate but not involved or, for that matter, involved but not intimate. He is both intimate and involved. A short summary showing that might be helpful.

Beginnings

In the first few verses of Genesis we read:

In the beginning when God created the heavens and the earth, the earth was a formless void and darkness covered the face of the deep, while a wind from God swept over the face of the waters. Genesis 1:1-2 (NRSV)

From that moment of intimate involvement in creation, we see the Spirit directly connected with life throughout the scriptures. As God 'speaks' through the creation narratives, so it is the wind or the 'breath' of the Spirit that carries his words. In the building of the Tabernacle and the Temple, it is the Spirit who enables and empowers various people to perform their tasks. From Bezalel and Oholiab[194] to the prophets and the seers, the Holy Spirit was empowering and intimately engaging in lives throughout the Old Testament narrative.

An unfolding story

In Genesis 6 we read of God's sober warning that his Spirit will not always strive with people. As one reads the pages of the Old Testament and follows the longings and yearnings of Israel, one sees a God who is nudging his people forward. Noah was guided by a dove (a symbol of the Holy Spirit); God spoke to Moses through a burning bush (fire being a symbol of the Spirit); when they were thirsty, God provide the Israelites with water (a symbol of the Holy Spirit); God led the Israelites with fire and cloud (both symbols of the Spirit);[195] when the kings of Israel were anointed, they were anointed with oil (a symbol of the Holy Spirit) and so the images and metaphors go on and on. The Holy Spirit can be seen and heard throughout the story of Israel.

Yet something happens as we journey through the Scriptures. Throughout the Old Testament there is also an ever increasing sense of promise that the Spirit will be even more intimately connected to and involved with the lives of God's people. God promises the people of Israel that he will take the law, which has been written on stones, and write it 'on their hearts'[196] and he promises that he will take away their heart of 'stone' and replace it with a heart of 'flesh'.[197] Through the prophet Joel he promises that there will be a day when he will 'pour out his Spirit on all flesh'[198] and he will give gifts to his people – special gifts such as visions and dreams and prophecy. The Old Testament closes with a yearning for this gift, a reaching out for this intimacy with God and his involvement in the lives of his people.

---

192   For both realities, see the Farewell Discourse in John 14-17.
193   See Ephesians 1.
194   See Exodus 31
195   These were the two main ways in which God led the children of Israel through the wilderness.
196   See Jeremiah 31, particularly v. 33.
197   See Ezekiel 36:26.
198   See Joel 2.

The New Testament

The New Testament opens with a flurry of Holy Spirit activity. This is particularly seen in the account of the births of both John the Baptist and Jesus in the Gospel of Luke.[199] The Spirit is the force by which Mary conceives.[200] The Spirit touches John the Baptist whilst he grows in Elizabeth's womb when the young Mary goes to see her cousin.[201] The Spirit causes both Anna and Simeon to prophesy.[202] It is the Holy Spirit that empowers Jesus and rests on him at his baptism.[203] It is the Spirit that forces Jesus into the wilderness to be tempted.[204] It is the Spirit that rests on him when he announces his manifesto in the Nazareth Synagogue.[205] The ministry of Jesus could not be understood without the intimacy and involvement of the Spirit.

When Jesus talks to Nicodemus,[206] he explains that the Holy Spirit is an untameable wind,[207] yet without him, conversion is not possible and life in God is inaccessible.[208] As Jesus prepares his disciples for the crucifixion, he talks to them about the centrality and the importance and the work of the Holy Spirit.[209] The Lord Jesus tells his disciples that the Spirit will guide them into all truth, he will convict them of sin, of righteousness and of judgement to come. He will defend them against the attacks of the enemy. He will empower them and nurture them. Yet he will also comfort them and give them assurance.

The birth of the Church and the early years

After Jesus' resurrection, he meets his disciples in Jerusalem and tells them that they are to wait there until they are empowered 'from on high'[210] then, on the Day of Pentecost, the Holy Spirit is poured out upon the church and the prophecy of Joel is fulfilled.[211] God is now indwelling his people by the power of the Holy Spirit. He is no longer resting on them temporarily, he is resident within them. And with that residency come both gifts of the Spirit[212] and the fruit of the Spirit which is evidence of increasingly Christ-like character and attitudes.[213] The Church in the New Testament is carried along by the wind of the Spirit, often trying to keep up with him as he pushes the Gospel of Jesus Christ out into the world. The New Testament closes with an invitation from the Holy Spirit to come and drink from his well and to meet the risen Christ.[214] The Holy Spirit continues to push the Church today. He continues to give gifts to God's people, to push us into new areas, to challenge us to think differently, to empower us for witnessing to Christ. He continues to shape the Church and to defend us from the enemy. As Paul warned the Ephesians, so we too must learn to fight our battles with spiritual weapons and to recognize that we face a dangerous foe.[215]

We are as dependent upon him now as we have always been. Without him, our faith becomes dry and lifeless, like the valley of dry bones in the vision of Ezekiel[216] but with him, we can advance the Kingdom of God and further the purposes of Christ.

---

199   See Luke 1-3.
200   See Luke 1:35.
201   See Luke 1:41.
202   See Luke 2:25-39.
203   See Luke 3:21-23.
204   See Luke 4:1.
205   See Luke 4:16ff.
206   See John 3.
207   See John 3:8.
208   See John 3:3,7.
209   See John 14-17.

---

210   See Acts 1:4,8.
211   See Acts 2 and Joel 2.
212   1 Corinthians 12; Romans 12; Ephesians 4 etc.
213   See Galatians 5.
214   See Revelation 22.
215   See Ephesians 6.
216   See Ezekiel 37.

The creative and controversial Spirit?

There is a sense in which the Holy Spirit also brings with himself an air of controversy precisely because he is so creative. Since God always communicates with us via his Spirit, his instructions to the Prophets must necessarily have been conduited through the work of the third person of the Trinity. There were times when those instructions were unorthodox! Hosea was commanded to marry a prostitute, and buy her back when she leaves, as a symbol of God's commitment to unfaithful Israel. Jeremiah, Ezekiel and Isaiah were all instructed to either say unconventional things or carry out unconventional prophetic acts. In the New Testament, Peter was pushed beyond the comfort zone of his Judaism and Paul was completely changed by his encounter with the Holy Spirit. But no other story is quite so unconventional as the Virgin birth, where Mary and Joseph had their whole lives turned upside down as a result of the working of the Holy Spirit. Are we confident enough in our relationship with God and our 'familiarity' with the Holy Spirit to allow him to disrupt our orderly lives with his creative, and sometimes controversial, instructions or have we boxed him in? We can, so often, conduct our Christian lives with God the Holy Spirit as a bystander. If we continue to do that, we begin to become acclimatized to his apparent absence – and that is the point at which decay sets in.

I am not sure that one can have an intimate, open and involved relationship with and dependency upon the Holy Spirit without that also carrying some level of unpredictability and 'danger'. How many churches or Christians have missed a moment for creativity and confident engagement with our culture because of the fear of controversy or the inability to 'hear' what the Holy Spirit is saying?

The Church as a creative, controversial, intimate and involved community

The reality is that if we only ever do what we have always done, we will only ever get what we have always had. There may be danger and risk involved with following the Spirit's leading and there may be unpredictability, but there will also be life! Too often we rush to the question, 'Is it safe?' before we ask the much more important question, 'Is it God?' We cannot discover a new ocean without being willing to lose sight of the shore first.

You can read more about risk and creativity in *Risk Takers*, which was published in 2013.[217] In it, I ask the fundamental question of whether or not we are willing to risk our name, reputation and legacy for the Kingdom of God and then set out eight key 'risks' for Christians to take today:

1. Step into the unstoppable story – recognize that God is the hero of our lives, not us.

2. Believe a bigger Gospel – allow the Gospel to be as big as God intended it to be. It impacts everything.

3. Say 'Yes' to Jesus – whatever he asks, whenever he asks it.

4. Follow where God leads – even if you don't quite understand.

5. Do the right thing not the easy thing – even if it makes you unpopular.

6. Live in the Niagara of Grace – God is much better at forgiving us than we are at accepting his forgiveness. We can cut ourselves off from a sense of his purpose by undermining his ability to deal with our failures.

7. Move beyond vampire Christianity – we have absolutely got to realise one fundamental reality – this is not about us! The blood and grace of God is not for us to enjoy at the expense of the rest of the world.

8. Let the future shape us – it is only as we allow the Spirit to give us a vision of the future which is more compelling than our status quo that we can find the courage to move forward.

217 DUNCAN, Malcom, Risk Takers: Living As God Intended (Oxford: Monarch, 2013).

How do the intimacy and the involvement of the Spirit give us confidence?

A glance at the biblical story makes it clear that the Third Person of the Trinity is present throughout the unfolding of God's purposes – but how does that help you or me to live out our Christian lives today? What difference does it make for us that the Spirit is here? Before addressing these questions, it might be helpful to think about the difference between 'arrogance' and 'confidence' and to think about ways in which we might behave arrogantly in the name of the Holy Spirit and how we might avoid that.

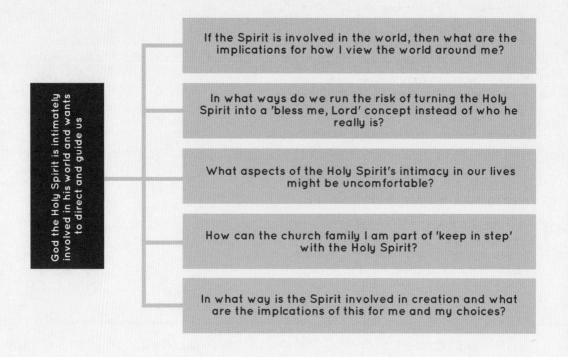

God the Holy Spirit is intimately involved in his world and wants to direct and guide us

If the Spirit is involved in the world, then what are the implications for how I view the world around me?

In what ways do we run the risk of turning the Holy Spirit into a 'bless me, Lord' concept instead of who he really is?

What aspects of the Holy Spirit's intimacy in our lives might be uncomfortable?

How can the church family I am part of 'keep in step' with the Holy Spirit?

In what way is the Spirit involved in creation and what are the implcations of this for me and my choices?

Further questions for personal reflection or group discussion:

As you reflect on what you have been exploring this week, are there specific areas of your life or ministry where you know you need to be strengthened in confidence?

What is your greatest longing for the work of the Spirit in your heart or in your community?

What is your biggest fear about the work of the Holy Spirit?

Transformation: two simple equations

So we are left with the clear picture from Scripture and the Church's history that the Holy Spirit is intimately involved in the world and in our lives. When you combine the intimacy of the Spirit in our lives and in the lives of others with the involvement of the Spirit in our world, our Christian communities and our own experiences, you end up with a potent cocktail of empowerment and transformation. One way of understanding the links between intimacy, involvement and empowerment and transformation is to set out a couple of simple equations. Sometimes I find such an approach helpful because it simplifies what could otherwise be a complicated issue.

Intimacy that leads to empowerment

1. *Intimacy* with ME means that the Spirit knows me completely - my weaknesses and my strengths.

2. *Intimacy* with the WORLD around me means that the Spirit knows what the needs around me are completely.

3. *Openness* to GOD means he can match my strengths with the needs around me, if I let him.

Involvement that leads to empowerment

1. *Involvement* with ME means that the Spirit is able to guide my steps, my thinking, my decisions, my resources and my life.

2. *Involvement* with the WORLD around me means that the Spirit is able to create opportunities and spaces as he sees fit.

3. *Openness* to the HOLY SPIRIT enables me to experience his empowerment.

Now let's take the ideas of intimacy, involvement, openness and empowerment and link them:

$$\text{Intimacy} + \text{Involvement} = \text{Empowerment}$$

$$\text{Empowerment} + \text{Openness} = \text{Transformation}$$

And now let's link transformation to our overarching theme of confidence.

Empowerment that leads to confidence

1. Because one of the characteristics of the Spirit is that he will guide me into TRUTH, I can be confident in the knowledge that as I read Scripture and seek to put God first, the Holy Spirit will not lead me into error.

2. Because the Spirit defends me against attacks of the enemy, I can be confident that as I walk in God's ways and seek to put him first, I will also walk in victory and wisdom.

3. Because the Spirit also has a role to convict me when I sin or lose sight of God's plans, I can be confident that he will show me the areas of my life that need to change and how to change them so that I become more effective in my service for Christ.

What is the Holy Spirit saying to the Church?

The Charismatic Movement was birthed in the late 1950s and early 1960s. Since then, its influence has grown across the world. Together with Pentecostalism, the Charismatic Movement has strengthened and blessed churches around the world as it has sought to hold onto the distinctive attribute of openness to the Holy Spirit. However, there is also a danger that the Charismatic Movement could become introverted if it is not careful. Consider the following quote from Michael Green's book, *I Believe In The Holy Spirit*, which he wrote in 1985.

No movement in Christendom should exist for itself. If it does so, it deserves to die, and it will not long be of service to the wider church. A spiritual movement is a signpost to what the whole Church should be like. Thus Catholicism should not be a denomination or a party, but a powerful exhibition of and pointer to that wholeness which Christ wills for all his people. Evangelicalism should not be a party within Christendom, or a subculture spanning the denominations. It is, at its best, a pointer to that loving outreach with the New Testament gospel of Christ which should characterize all God's people. Equally, the charismatic movement has little to offer if it is just a body of enthusiasts at a particular stage in history, but everything to offer if it demonstrates to the Church universal that dependence on the grace of God, that expectancy of his active intervention, which marked out the earliest Christians but is all too rare nowadays. The future of the charismatic movement lies not in itself but in its faithfulness in so embodying the charismatic life of the Spirit that this overflows into the whole Church.
Michael Green, *I Believe In The Holy Spirit*[218]

There is a profound challenge here. Is it possible that the Holy Spirit himself is challenging the part of the Church that seeks to be most open to him, to be careful not to become obsessed with him? Michael Green warned the charismatic church of the dangers of introversion and self-absorption when he first wrote *I Believe In The Holy Spirit*. Have we listened to that warning or do we need to consider again whether we are focusing too much on ourselves and not enough on the world around us?

---

218   GREEN, Michael, I Believe In The Holy Spirit (London: Hodder, 1985) pp. 292-293.

Spiritual Myopia
Try using this poem as a prayer [219]

We need healing, Lord!
Our spiritual myopia
Is eroding our vision
of a bigger plan.
So the inevitable
Collision
Of our church Utopia
With the limited
scope it has
Is making us
more comfortable
than we should be.

Our ground is getting smaller,
So we get a bigger crowd
but on a smaller space
And we make the music loud
enough to drown out the cries
of the broken and the poor.

Bigger congregations
won't answer segregation.
Locking ourselves in prayer
won't show that we care.
Enjoying when we meet
won't change the street.
Becoming more respectable
won't change the spectacle
Of communities that need
Hope infused
Sin refused
Tension defused
Satan confused
Saints enthused.

We need healing, Lord.
New eyes to see
New ears to hear
That You are here!

Faith to believe that You win.
Courage to push the envelope
Until You envelop
People
Streets
Communities
Towns
Nations
Continents
And turn the world
Right way up.

We don't need bigger buildings
We need bigger hearts.
We don't need to increase our capacity for seats,
We need to increase our capacity to love.
We don't need more blessing
We need to be blessing more.
We don't need more grace,
We need to be more gracious.
We don't need more of God,
God needs more of us.
There isn't an answer around the corner
We are the answers hiding in a corner.
God doesn't need to fit into our plans
We need to fit into God's

And His plan is change from the inside out.
Hope from the foetus of faith
To the adulthood of the Kingdom
Courage that pushes us out
Birthing pangs that scream a declaration
Through the heavenlies
HE IS HERE.

God won in the Jerusalem dirt
When Christ was planted
Like a seed in the ground
Beside Golgotha's mound
And three days later
The Seed pushed through the earth...
The plant has been growing ever since
And we are now Its seed
Called to germinate
To propagate, to profligate the Gospel.
God wins.

219 'Spiritual Myopia' © Malcolm Duncan 2011.

The challenge of the Spirit to the Church

It would seem clear that the Holy Spirit is always pushing the church into new areas. He is given to us for many reasons, some of which we have explored, but one of the central reasons for his *indwelling* us (which is not surprising given the call upon God's people that tells us we are blessed to be a blessing) is that we might engage *missionally* with the world around us.

The Holy Spirit is intimately involved in the world and in our lives – but we must be open to his empowerment *for service and mission* if we are to make a lasting impression for Christ. John Howard Yoder wrote *The Politics Of Jesus* in 1972, and in it he argued that the Church had the responsibility to discern where God was working in the world and join him in that task.[220] The great challenge for any local church, indeed the great challenge for any Christian, is to *allow* the Holy Spirit to lead us into new things or new places.

We are creatures of habit and, if left to our own devices, we will often opt for the familiar, the known and the predictable. That is not always for bad reasons, but the challenge still remains that we must embrace the direction and the leading of the Spirit *into* and now *away from* the world if we are to make a lasting difference in our society. It is only as we discover how to be Spirit-led in our outlook on the world and our mission in our society that we will make a difference.

There are some Spirit-led opportunities that we have in our generation to make a lasting difference for the Kingdom of God. For example, the opportunity to provide community spaces with our buildings; the opportunities to engage in a new generation of apologetics; the opportunities of providing education; the opportunities for engagement with people from different faiths; the opportunities to be distinctively and clearly Christian and biblical in the areas of ethics, morality and social norms. The question is not whether the opportunities are there or not. The question is whether we are brave enough to take them.

---

220   YODER, John Howard, The Politics Of Jesus: Behold The Man!
Our Victorious Lamb (Carlisle: Paternoster, 1994).

What are the opportunities that the Spirit is nudging you into?

We very often 'privatise' the voice and work of the Holy Spirit and seek his will and purpose on our own, or away from the wider picture of what God is doing in the world. That is not a helpful way of discerning the Spirit's voice. John repeatedly quotes the Lord Jesus in Revelation with the phrase, 'He who has an ear, let him hear what the Spirit is saying to the churches.'

If we want to discern what God is saying to us, we must start with what his overarching purposes and plans are and fit in with them, rather than asking him to fit in with our plans.

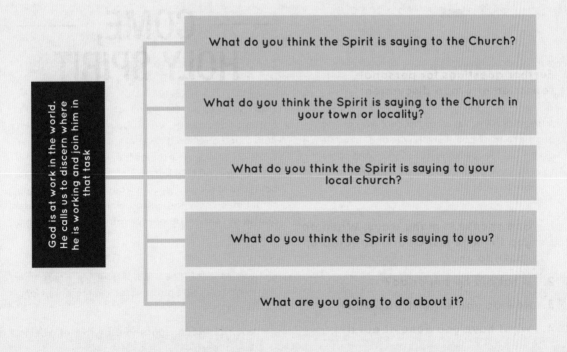

God is at work in the world. He calls us to discern where he is working and join him in that task

What do you think the Spirit is saying to the Church?

What do you think the Spirit is saying to the Church in your town or locality?

What do you think the Spirit is saying to your local church?

What do you think the Spirit is saying to you?

What are you going to do about it?

Each evening, during our celebrations, we will be inviting you to go beyond 'studying' the issue we have been facing each day and to enter into an encounter with God. To do that, we will be using Jesus' powerful words of hope, comfort and challenge to his disciples contained in his parting address to them. This is known as The Farewell Discourse and is found in the Gospel of John in chapters 14-17. We will also be using Psalm 46 to help us encounter God.

Why not take a few moments either before or after the evening celebration, to reflect on the words of both of these passages and to ask God to either prepare you for what he wants to do in your life and heart or to confirm what he has done as you prepare to sleep.

COME, HOLY SPIRIT

This evening, as we focus on the Holy Spirit's presence and power, we will be reflecting on Psalm 46:6-7 and on John 16. We will also be considering some of the powerful things that God is doing in his Church around the world. Stories of courage and boldness and confidence always inspire us – they sometimes challenge us too. Think through these questions either before or after this evening's celebrations:

- Where is the one area of your life where you need the Holy Spirit to break in more than any other?

- What barriers might there be to him moving in that area?

- How can you remove those barriers so that he can move?

Further questions for personal reflection or group discussion:

A friend of mine has a very helpful way of enabling people to think about their lives and ministries. He asks them the following questions. Take some time to reflect on them yourself, or with others, as you prepare to return home:

1. **God speaks in many ways. When do you think he last clearly directed or spoke to you?**

2. **What did he say or do?**

3. **How do you know it was God?**

4. **What have you done about it?**

Lord,

Give me the confidence
to break new ground for you.
Give me the boldness to leave behind old ways.
Help my yearning for change to be stronger than
my attachment to what has been.
Let my frustration with the status quo outweigh
my apathy.

Give me fresh confidence in who you are.
Give me fresh confidence in what you want to do
in the world.
Give me fresh confidence in what my part
in your plan is.

Teach me to take risks, not to avoid them.
Enable me to try,
even if I fail.

Let my life count for you.

Amen

—— GOD'S CONFIDENCE IN US ——

And so we come to the end of our exploration of confidence.

We began the journey by looking at our confidence in God. We can trust him because he has proven himself reliable, faithful and good. He never lets his people down.

We have walked through the truths at the heart of our faith as captured by the Apostles' Creed. We've explored the confidence that flows from a Father who is personal and powerful; the confidence we can have in the Son who is tangible, tender and transforms us and the confidence we can have in the Spirit who is intimate and involved in our lives.

But what if we turn the tables? What if we think about God's confidence in us? It is hard to believe, but he has chosen you and me to be his conduits of love and grace into the world around us. He has given us the resources that we need, the assurance of his grace and the way in which we are to go about this great task. We are to 'go into all the world and make disciples'. We are not just to make a difference, we are not just to be nice people. We are to make disciples.

God entrusts us with the greatest privilege imaginable. The opportunity to be his hands, feet and voice into our culture, our society and our community.

To stand up.

To reach out.

To speak out for the poor, the marginalized and the excluded.

To tell the truth.

To share the story of Jesus.

To take the risk.

We'll fail. We'll falter. We'll struggle and we'll wonder if we will get there
but God makes this promise: I'll be with you every step of the way.[221]

We really can change the world.

Best get started...

---

221   See Matthew 28:20